DAVID L. KING

LOOKING BACK
THROUGH **The CRACK**

From Crack Fiend to Millionaire God Let Him Live

Looking Back Through The Crack
From Crack Fiend to Millionaire God Let Him Live
Copyright © 2019 by David L. King

Library of Congress Control Number: 2019908168
ISBN-13: Paperback: 978-1-950073-58-0
        ePub: 978-1-950073-59-7

All rights reserved. No part of this publication may be reproduced, distributed, or transmitted in any form or by any means, including photocopying, recording, or other electronic or mechanical methods, without the prior written permission of the publisher or author, except in the case of brief quotations embodied in critical reviews and certain other noncommercial uses permitted by copyright law.

Although every precaution has been taken to verify the accuracy of the information contained herein, the author and publisher assume no responsibility for any errors or omissions. No liability is assumed for damages that may result from the use of information contained within.

Printed in the United States of America

GoToPublish LLC
1-888-337-1724
www.gotopublish.com
info@gotopublish.com

Contents

Chapter 1	The Early Years	1
Chapter 2	The Good And The Bad Turned Ugly	15
Chapter 3	The transition! Came as quite a surprise!	29
Chapter 4	I became a substance abuser	31
Chapter 5	J.R. Jake and Matt	51
Chapter 6	My 6th program	55
Chapter 7	Living Life On It's Own Terms	59
Chapter 8	"A new job"	63
Chapter 9	"Meeting the Warrior Queen"	67
Chapter 10	A new homeowner!	79
Chapter 11	The year 2000	95

CHAPTER 1

The Early Years

I, David King, HAD the greatest pleasure of my life; meeting and marrying the warrior queen; but this amazing story will begin with me.

I was raised in San Mateo California. I was raised within a family of seven by Teresa, Nate and four other siblings. San Mateo during the early years was a city that had the American so-called melting pot. Just on my block alone there were many different races of people. We were an African-American family. Our neighbors, from memory were Chinese, Mexican, African-American, Caucasian, Filipino etc. and of course there could have been more cultures that I didn't know of. I felt like San Mateo was one of the greatest places I could have grown up in. The weather was excellent.

San Mateo was about 30 miles south of San Francisco. It was 40 miles south of San Jose; and about 30 to 40 miles east of Oakland. At one time as a kid I remember San Mateo County was rated the second richest county in the nation. Our family would never have been classified as well to do though. If I were to describe our economic status, I would call it upper lower class. We never classified ourselves as poor; yet we definitely didn't call ourselves rich either. We never lacked for anything. I was a very fortunate young man. Nate was a workaholic and fixed everything himself. He had great ability. Teresa worked as a maid early on; and was a very loving person.

Nate was the backbone of our household. Teresa put in work no doubt, but Nate was the breadwinner. During my early years before the age of 10; Nate was a construction worker; a foreman. He drove the company truck home. It had a two-way radio in it. I thought that was so cool. This was in the 1960s; way before the dawn of cell phones. Nate, from the stories he told me, grew up with a strong work ethic; which was passed on to most of his kids; by the way. Nate was a farmer during his early years. He had, I believe eight siblings. Somebody had to work the farm while his siblings went to school. Therefore he only had a sixth grade education. Yet he managed to raise a family of seven, until all the siblings were grown. I will always be forever grateful for the sacrifices he made for our family. He was a great man. He passed away in 2005. Wow! What a great man. He taught me how to become a man.

Even though I didn't become that man, for many years to come, I watched him in action daily. That man never seemed to sweat anything. He was always composed. He had great wit. That's what the old folks would say about a person that had great natural ability, talent and great common sense. There were a lot of old sayings, like a bird in the hand is worth two in the bush. I don't know if that's in the bible are not. But it was one of the sayings that were passed down. For those that don't know; it means that one bird that's in your hand that you can see and feel is worth more than the two birds in the bush that you can't see. Nate gave me the staying power that I would need over 40 years later to be in position to be the man for the warrior queen. This man's strength is what I remember and tapped into to give me the strength and staying power, to be in position to be a real man; for my queen.

I must spend more time on this man because he was the man. I am a product of his genes. When the queen needed me I stepped up at her most needed hour. I was in position, not to glorify myself, but to give honor to the man before myself.

In the early years it was because of Nate's position as a construction foreman that carried the financial day.

Teresa was a good God fearing woman. Before I was born, she had two off-springs from a previous marriage. By the way moms and pops were never married. Yes my mom's had two off-springs when she met Nate. They then had three more including me.

Pops was a medium height man. He stood 5 feet 10 or 11. He had much wit and a great sense of humor. He was not a drinker or did drugs. He did tell me that he had been an alcoholic years before I was born. He told me of how he knew how to make moonshine alcohol when he was a kid. He told me he knew how to make the red and the white moonshine. During my whole life of knowing him I saw him take maybe three drinks. Not a drinker.

Teresa was great especially during the early days. She had to walk 33 blocks to go to work in the morning as a maid. At that time in San Mateo the buses were not running that often. Nate started work very early. Teresa got us kids off to school, cleaned the house, and began her walk to work in her white uniform. She worked for a lady and would tell us horror stories that the lady told her. My mother retold to us the atrocities perpetrated by the evil in her country, to her employers people.

Stories were told her about how political misfits would have their army round up and hurt her people; and make lampshades with their skin. Moms never learned to drive; therefore pops did all the driving. She was a very loving person with a Baptist religious background. Her Old Man was a preacher. I think his Old Man was too. She was very serious about her religion. As kids she would take us to Pilgrim Baptist Church in San Mateo. I would not know for years later that my queen would have the same temperament as my Teresa; who was a queen in her own right. Yes way back then, Nate gave me the genes and the script of what a real man was. Moms gave me the initial example of what I would search for in my queen.

Teresa had a very strong religious foundation; early before my age of 10. What happened around that time? Perhaps I will never know what truly happened to change her; but change she did. She started to drink and drink often. Moms is moms, you know. I will always love Teresa; but I don't know what triggered her habit. It could have been something Nate did; because she started to cuss at that man. It seemed like at least twice a week she would drink and cuss at that man. That man, my dad, the man. I never understood what he did. Even to this day over 40 years later. I can only speculate. Perhaps there is a clue in the fact that I left something out concerning Nate.

Nate was married previously before meeting Teresa. As previously stated she had two off-springs when she met Nate. Nate also had off-spring from a previous relationship. Nate was previously married to a woman in Fresno California. He had two biological off-springs and more he had an attachment to; that may or may not have been his. I really don't know for sure, which ones were biological or not; because back at that time I was not yet a teenager. I do know that some of the ones in the household in Fresno, before Teresa, were not his biological off-spring. But he took on the responsibility while he was there with his previous woman. There was a breakup. I don't know what it was. Maybe they both were to blame. Nate and his woman separated. There was one son that took this breakup very hard; because he was left without Nate. That feeling burned in his heart.

I first met this sibling of mine very early. From what I can remember when I was 10 or 11 years old. This young man of about 17 or 18 came north to the bay area to see Nate.

I had met him and the rest of Nate's relations extremely early in my life at perhaps the age of six or seven years old; when Nate drove us all the 200 miles south to attend a funeral in Fresno. I don't remember who passed away. But at that age I was too young to remember who was who. This young man came to the bay area looking for Nate. Nate was not in this young man's life; and he was very bitter in his heart. He showed no outward signs of bitterness in his demeanor when he came to the bay. But nevertheless I felt the anger and bitterness 40 years later.

Teresa maybe had sadness and anger over something he did. Maybe he cheated.

Maybe he was tipping out with the former woman he had. Maybe I will never know for sure. Yet she started drinking. She cussed at that man mostly while she was not sober.

That man was like God himself to me. That man who never, ever called anyone to fix anything. He had great talents. He fixed everything. When the dishwasher went out, he fixed it. When the washing machine or dryer broke down he fixed it. He put a roof on the house by himself. He built a deck in the backyard by himself. He did it all by himself.

This great man was being cussed at constantly. I couldn't understand it as a youngster. I will always love both of them though. Even so, mom's alcoholic outbursts put a lot of emotional strain upon me. I didn't find out for years later what impact it had upon me. I remember this man never put hands on her; and never cussed her back. He just left, and came back to be about his work daily. I don't want to paint him as a saint. And I don't want to paint my mother as nothing but a raging alcoholic. Maybe she had reason to treat him like that. I just didn't have the knowledge about the situation.

There was a great impact on myself. That impact was the fact that I couldn't bring friends to the household, at least inside. I never knew if she was going to start drinking or not any given day. There were many times when she would go on a drinking rampage and called the ambulance with all the bells, whistles and lights flashing.

Neighbors would stand outside and watch, noticing that she was obviously drunk. One week in particular she called the ambulance twice in a week. It was very embarrassing to me as a young boy. I would find out later that it impacted me greatly. Yet I'll always love Teresa and Nate. This day December 2015 they are both gone to glory. My mom's passed away in 1997. My dad passed away in 2005. I will always love them and miss them dearly.

Bernice was very special and loving to me. She was seven years older than I was. She was also the only girl in the household in the bay area. I did get to know two other siblings from Nate's previous relationship later. But at this time, in my household, she was the only girl. Bernice grew to become my very best friend. I loved her greatly. She passed away in 1994. Bernice as far as I remember had no known enemies. She was cool. She had great integrity and was smart; also hip. She helped me with my clothes and prepared my meals when my mom was unable. She was a great person at heart. She left the household when I was a teenager. She met a man from Milwaukee Wisconsin. His name was DC. He was a kind man as far as I remember in the beginning. They had three boys and one girl. The girl was a firstborn. She had a different Old Man. The three boys were all from the man from Wisconsin. Bernice will always be in my heart as my friend, my sibling and my love would never fade for her. Even though Bernice was not Nate's daughter he raised her from about the age of four or five years old until she was grown. Her old man, lived in the same city. He was very cool; and had great style. His name was Jerome.

I would visit him now and then as a teenager. I was always welcomed and profited also from his knowledge.

My oldest sibling Mark was the first thug I even knew way back then. That was before the word thug became a national term. Mark was a good-looking guy and the women took notice.

Before all the penitentiaries, I remember when I first lost my oldest sibling from our little family circle; and the bay area. He was 14 years old and I was nine. I don't remember what he did. But I do know it was something serious. Nate was going to lay hands on him, and discipline him; before Mark started to run. Nate raised this young man since he was three or four years old. This of course was not his biological son; but it was Nate that raised him. I remember clearly my sister yell out "Run Mark run". He did run. He ran out the door and out of my life. This started a life of juvenile's and crime. I never truly knew Mark from that time on. He roamed from house to house. He became trouble man. We would get periodic meetings and sightings of him in the future' but it was usually trouble.

I do remember one time after Mark had run away, Nate found out where he was.

Nate went out and bought sheriff hats, gun belts, guns and badges; for Arnold and myself. He took us to the place where Mark was. He told me at the age of nine and my youngest sibling; at the age of seven, that Mark would be running out the backyard of the house that we were at. Nate went to the door.

There I was with Arnold and I dressed like an old west sheriff and his deputy; waiting for the bad guy to run to us. Sure enough within a couple of minutes Mark came running out the back gate right past his two younger siblings. I often wonder what he thought, seeing his two younger siblings there to detain him, as he ran past. Nate had an incredible sense of humor.

This was in the 70s and 80s. But my setbacks will be explained in later chapters. I will always love Mark, and hope to see him again one day. I hope he is still alive. Yet I'm not prepared to look on the streets of Oakland California for him.

I have enough sense not to do that.

The next youngest son was Nate's actual biological son in the bay area. His name was J.R. J.R was very studious early on. Just like Bernice, he was smart and stable. J.R and Bernice graduated high school and moved on with their lives.

J.R went on to be very good at accounting and bookkeeping. He was very kind to me as a older sibling. He was my first definition of a cool square, as I will later call myself. I looked as a youngster at Mark and his way with the ladies. He ran the streets and survived. He was cool, and I wanted to be cool. J.R. was more of a square; but was very smart and studious. He got good jobs and was about his business. I wanted to be just like both of them. Early on I set my sights unknowingly as being a cool square.

Yet I was more square than cool. This was like taboo in the black community. A square was looked upon as someone strange. I didn't have street smarts or street savvy, and I stood out like a sore thumb.

I was the next youngest. Yet I will mention that there was another sibling that was younger than I. Nate's youngest off-spring. His name was Arnold. Arnold was not a big thinker. He kind of reacted to life around him. He was my youngest sibling, and we were separated by almost 2 years. Although we were close in age, we were not as close as we could have been. I don't know if he ever graduated high school or not. I remember us playing as little kids. We played a lot in the front yard, and the backyard. Those of course were the good old days. Yes we had, I thought a very typical upbringing. Love was there because moms and pops did their job. We were protected, cared for and loved. They did their job. Love was present but was not shown openly. I never saw my moms and pops even embrace ever.

    I guess it made me, not such a sensitive person. That upbringing shaped me and gave me the foundation to go on with the rest of my life; with the good and the bad. I will say that they did us a favor; by setting up our living situation in the bay area. I loved that city. I was very fortunate to have been raised in a non-ghetto situation. There were no obvious gang situations going on in my city. There were of course underground gangs that were not in the overwhelming public sight; and of course out of my sight. I have no horror stories to tell about the early stages of my upbringing, at least concerning gangs.

    That was not a concern for me.

    Pop was getting verbally abused quite often during my teen years by my mom's. I was very proud of him as a man. He took the verbal abuse from my mother's drinking state and never retaliated. He never put hands on her. He could have physically smacked her up; or verbally smashed her; but he did not. He simply took it and went about his business. I asked him later why he took so much from her. "There is something to be said about love". That's what he told me. I know he loved her or he would not have taken so much from her. At the same time I truly believe that he took it because he wanted to make sure he was there for his kids. At this time the two oldest siblings had moved out. Mark was in and out of penitentiaries. Bernice had moved to her own place a block away. I think deep in Nate's heart he regretted that he wasn't there for his kids from his previous woman in Fresno. I think that's why he stayed and took the negativity from Teresa. He didn't want to let his kids down that he had in my household in the bay area. I am grateful that he stayed: because at this time he was the only wage earner that was contributing to the household. My mom was starting to have physical problems, and if he left Arnold and I would have been devastated. He gave me the foundation to rise into manhood. I wanted to give the foundation of myself, so as to let it be known that the staying power I used for the warrior Queen some 40 years later was given to me by the first man in my life; by Nate. Oh by the way, Nate used to say when I was a teenager that he would leave Teresa and get him a white woman; when me and my younger brother, were grown, and out of the house. He never did get that white woman, but he did leave her; when his last two off-springs, left the household. He did make sure Teresa got her disability started. Because after the early years of moms walking so far to work each day; she had gotten two broken legs on her left side and one broken leg on her right side. She ended up having both legs cut off; and ended up in a care facility. This is where she passed away in 1997; after her daughter in 1994.

I don't know what pops was thinking, but he dated and lived with Aunt Laura.

This hurt Teresa greatly. But she never spoke about it to me. I don't understand his thinking. To this day over 10 years after he has passed, that will forever be the only blemish I have of my memory of Nate. My aunt moved to the bay area from Houston Texas. She stayed with us for a little while. I ended up getting arrested for some stupid stuff. When I returned after 90 days they were an item.

Late into my teenage years, Aunt Laura moved to our house from Texas. At that time Nate was no longer a construction worker. He was a hustler; a legal hustler though.

Nate was an honest man in dealing with life in the general public. I never witnessed him getting arrested ever. He just had too many talents to put in place. He remodeled old houses, and did hauling. He had many contacts from his years as a construction man.

He worked on the San Mateo Bridge; which at one time was classified as the longest bridge in the world. Nate suffered a series of illness's years later. Those physical issues took away his construction career. Aunt Laura used to work with him remodeling old houses and I guess that's when their romance developed. Yeah I know viewing from the outside it seems wrong; but it happened. Shortly after she came to live with us and started working with him, I got locked up for the first time.

Before I speak about my first time in jail I will give background of myself; who was not yet seasoned. I was always overweight of course, until the drug addict days which will be discussed in later chapters. I was overweight from my earliest years. I allowed this to cause me great problems in my early life; and into adulthood. I remember as a young kid, at six years old, my younger sibling and I would pretend to be Batman and Robin. We would tie towels to our backs and run around the backyard yelling "Batman! Batman!" Arnold ran through a hole in the fence, and I followed. I got stuck in the fence and had to yell for someone to get me loose. I was a loner because I couldn't bring friends over to my house because of Teresa's drinking issues. I was a loner because I had low self-esteem. I was lonely and did a lot of living in my own mind. I did not love myself. I didn't even like myself. I had a lot of self-loathing going on. I was also very dark-skinned. I felt at that time like the lighter one is, the better one is. I felt unattractive in that dark skin. I once looked in the mirror as a youth and said to myself "you're fat, black and ugly". A lot of self-loathing flowed through my veins. I couldn't wear any of the stylish clothes the kids my age were wearing. The old man pants that I had to wear were always too long; so they had to be altered. I wore a size 40 pants at the age of 12. I was a bully early on in grade school. If you were having a ball game in the physical education period at school, and the ball bounced away. And it got to me. I would kick the ball to the other side of the field. I was not happy in my life back then. I hated myself for being fat, black and ugly. I was very miserable inside; although I felt my upbringing was adequate. I'll be forever grateful for my parents; for giving me a chance, with a foundation for life. I just needed to gain experience and figure it out for myself.

 I was bussed to a pretty much all white school during the late 60s. My neighborhood was mixed, yes but the few friends I had in the neighborhood were black. At that time in the neighborhood and among my friends, it was cool to be cool. I really wasn't cool at that time. What I acquired was a good educational foundation. That educational foundation would later help me greatly. I did go to college later which was one of the greatest decisions I could have made for myself. But that will be discussed later. I wanted to describe my upbringing a little bit before getting to the later chapters, with the warrior queen.

 Unlike my older sibling Mark, I was not good with the ladies. My self-esteem was shot; because of the constant put downs and negative thoughts I put upon myself. I was a basket case. I felt fat, black, low self-esteem, ugly and not cool. Constant self-loathing, self-doubt and negative feelings stayed with me for years. I become extremely good at basketball. I got a job at a rec center where I played a lot of basketball. I was good, real good. On the court, I would stop my dribble on purpose and call my defender to stick me. No one could block my shot; and I was excellent! I had a shot like the old former warrior and Laker Jamar Wilkes. I loved basketball. It was my therapy, although all these emotional issues were going on within me. I still rallied around education. My parents helped me to know that education was extremely important. I had good work ethic. At the ages of about 9, 10 and 11 three siblings myself, J.R. and Arnold all had paper routes.

 We worked for the San Francisco Chronicle. The deliveryman would drop the newspapers on our porch around 3:30 or 4:30AM.

 We would awake before 4 AM; fold and go out to deliver our papers, on bikes in the early morning. On Sundays when the papers were perhaps five to six times bigger. Nate would drop the papers along our routes, fitted in the extra paper route bags that we had.

Nate would drop the papers along our routes so that we would empty our paper route bags, and run right into another bag. When we all finished our routes around 7 AM or so, we would ride our bikes to a little café in downtown San Mateo called Jim's Donut Den. Every morning Nate would buy breakfast for us and we would interact with him. What does an 11-year-old do with $400 a month? I kept my money because of the work ethic I learned from him. I took that work ethic with me throughout my life. I got a regular job at 14 years old, leaving a paper route behind after three years of religiously handling my young business. At 14 there was something called the Ceta program in my county? I got a job painting the numbers on the sidewalks for addresses. At 16 I got a job at the Martin Luther King Recreation Center. I worked with an older man; perhaps he was about 54. Anyway he was in his 50s. His name was Joe. He sold me a 1967 Chevy Malibu for $500. Wow! I didn't know it was going to be a collector's item later in my life.

Therefore at 16, yeah I had a lot of negative traits going on. I had some self-loathing going on, except on the basketball court. I was very good. I grew only to be 5 foot 9 3/4; but I played much taller than that. Negative traits yeah, I was still overweight but an over achiever on the court. On the positive side I had good work ethic. I kept money, and was gaining a confidence as a good worker. I was still a square but my cool square days were ahead of me. I scored some cool points by getting the clean car. I was in a car club. I was the treasurer. We were a lowrider club. I put diamond tuck and plush carpet in my car. I became the treasurer because I had trustworthiness from my peers. I had not acquired the cool, savvy, hustle my peers had at that time because of their time on the streets. I was a working guy, a money guy; but I got my money from square jobs; not from street hustle. Many people envied me but I didn't know it because I envied them. I did not know at that time how much potential I had; or the foundation of talents that I was acquiring.

I had not put much time on the streets because I was cultivating my education.

Education and street smarts were two different things to me. Yes I acquired a car and I kept money, which made me envied by many; but I wanted that street savvy. Just like the guys seemed to be having all the fun and all the girls. Yeah, girls, I was still a virgin at 16. I didn't even have a clue. I saw guys that were obviously no good, get any girl they wanted. I just didn't have it. I had no conscious understanding about game. I know Mark had it; but I did not. I remember asking Mark one time, in hopes of getting some sort of info; some sort of game. What he did tell me was that if I didn't believe in myself, how I can I expect someone else to believe in me. Well years later I had belief in myself; enough to step to the warrior queen; but at this time, at the age of 16, I had much growing to do.

I did get a girlfriend at 16. She was 14 and already had more street savvy than myself.

She was also no longer pure. I took her home to meet Teresa, and moms did not like her. I guess Teresa knew best. She only wanted me for my car. She broke my heart a little bit near the end. And I got no intimacy from her. I mostly blamed myself. I just had no experience, and I didn't know how to show her how I felt.

One day I was walking to school because my car was down that day. I would walk about six blocks to my high school. I went to San Mateo high school. I walked past the Martin Luther King Junior recreation Center. A young man, a town misfit who was perhaps 20 or 21, called out to me from the bleachers of the baseball field. His real nickname was Ron. He called out "D.L." I answered who's that. He said" it's Ron. I smoked weed that day, and loved it. I've loved weed ever since. As they say weed is the gateway to other things. It was for me. I later went on at the age of 24 to be a substance abuser; such lowly beginnings for myself. But I would rise to power in later chapters. I would never again smoke weed before school. It just wasn't my thing to do. I did put my studies first. I was an average student with above average potential. I hated high school because I was a scrub. I didn't have a lot of friends. I was dealing with the self-loathing, low self-esteem and was constantly putting myself down. I was not real happy those days, most of the time. I did manage to gain a few so-called friends because I had the car. Those friends were not real friends though. They just liked my car. I played tackle football my freshman year. Although I was the biggest guy out there, of course I didn't have the speed to play any of the glamour positions. I always played on the line; defensive tackle.

I went to high school, lonely depressed and alone. No mates or, dates, a basket case. Yet I still had workaholic roots from Nate. Therefore I worked my way through—out high school. I still envied the street guys. And they envied me. They didn't have the education I had. Most of them would cut class, act out in class and fell short of a good education. That was not me. I did my school work and my money work.

One day I was selling weed outside of the rec center. I didn't know it yet but my street cred was about to get a thin foundation. Some thugs pulled up in a car. I was letting go of some weed. I got ripped off. I was furious. They must have driven around the corner. They came back and I shouted "where's my money"? Manny rolled the window halfway down, with a big smile on his face, and held up five dollars. I snatched the five dollars out his hand; and took five out on his nose. I hit him square on his nose. Blood was gushing out. Everyone was shocked including me. I realized immediately after that, that there was three of them and only one of me. Three doors flew open and I backed up, waiting for a three on one altercation. Instead of coming at me in triple, they went to the trunk. Manny came running toward me with confidence and a Jack. I backed up with him yelling and laughing. I ran with him chasing me. I stopped on a dime with him almost running into me. I grabbed the Jack from him before he realized what was happening. I swung the Jack back and forth approaching him. All the people around were laughing and then started yelling "drop the Jack, go toe to toe". I knew I had no backup out there. I knew this Jack gave me an advantage. Yet I figured I could take him. I did drop the jack. I guess he thought he could get the better of me. I'm sure he thought I was lame. I had not become known. I was not known on the streets and therefore a easy mark; I'm sure he thought.

We fought. I got the better of him. The fight was stopped by someone. Everyone listened to that person. No one was going to go against him. He was the age of Bernice; and no one was going to go against him. Perhaps he was making sure no one jumped me in numbers because I was the younger sibling of Bernice, his peer who he respected. I really don't know for sure why he intervened; but that was it. That was the day I got a measure of street cred.

Yeah I was a real scrub at that time socially. Yet academically I held my own. In the business world I was a good worker. It was very easy for me to get a job. I always rolled with money. Therefore at this age in life 16, 17 and going on 18 I did have some tools that were going to give me some solid foundation. My senior year in High school was more of the same socially. I have felt pressure within the black community because of the dark skin that I had. I would receive pressure from the white community because of my black skin. I never seemed to fit. I wasn't light enough. I felt that way back in grade school when I was busted to an all-white school. I would be the only black student in a lot of my classes. Most of the black students cut their classes. I never cut; I stayed in the middle of those classes and competed. I remember a class in fourth grade where I was excelling in reading. The teachers separated the students into levels of reading. I was in the middle level but pushing the top tier. I strongly felt that that teacher held me back from the top tier because of her unfairness.

If you're white, you're alright, if your brown stick around. If you're black get back. It was my unspoken reality, at that time, at that age. It wasn't a time of Jim Crow of course; but despite the new knowledge of black thought history and feelings that was constant in the 60s; to me this was a constant from inside and outside the race.

I didn't graduate high school normally, across the stage. In order to graduate high school, at my school in the community you had to pass swimming. I was ashamed of my fat body; therefore I didn't want to take swimming, or to care about knowing how to swim, at that time. I did take the C.H.S.C.P. E. It's called the California High School Proficiency Examination. It had no scores. It was basically a pass or fail ordeal. I passed; therefore I received an equivalent of my diploma around February of my senior year. I told Teresa and Nate I was done, and I rolled on. Yet the best thing I did was to go to college that coming September.

Chapter 2

The Good And The Bad Turned Ugly

NOW AT THE AGE of 18, I was the sum of all my parts; the good and the bad. I was now free of the restrictions of school; and I pondered my future. I looked at myself and saw my strengths as well as my weakness. Academically I felt like I could hold my own. I was a well-rounded student of the fundamentals of reading, writing and math. I was especially proficient in math and writing; for that matter also reading. I was content with that. The summer before beginning college in 1979, I concentrated on working. At my house, at that time, there were only Arnold and I; including Teresa and Nate.

Nate continued to do what he was doing; holding down the house. Teresa, now free of younger kid's duties, finally got a little break. Now that we were older.

Arnold and I, we were now independent of her because of our age.

I was somewhat apprehensive about starting college. I knew I had been a scrub in high school. I knew I hated high school with a passion. I didn't have any idea what college would be like. My social life was a joke. I was still pure at the age of 18.

I didn't have a clue. I was a very honest person at that time; to my core. Yes, that would slowly change. Even though at that time, that was the core foundation of who I was. I found that the world was not honest to its core. At least the world as it affected me. The streets were definitely not honest. The streets that I thought I would love so much was not honest. The games, the excitement, the hustle and the women. I saw the exciting part of street life. I had a little inside knowledge of the other parts. The lockups penitentiaries, probation and parole. I just ran with the idea that I really would like to be cool; and I wasn't. I did see the other side somewhat. I remember all the trouble Mark had gotten into. I never thought that would happen to me. I wanted a taste of the excitement, the girls, the laughter, the fun.

I remember the first day of college. I was now an official student at the College of San Mateo. I was excited. It was pretty cool. The atmosphere was laid-back. I was a business major. I really liked my business courses. I found college to be very easy. My first semester I had a B average, I began to love college. I didn't feel like a scrub. I felt empowered. There were young man and women from all over the world. I fit in nicely. I felt such freedom heading to the college campus every day. At this time my junior college career was going just fine. I worked while going to college. I held various jobs; always good jobs, for a young man working his way through college. I would now get most of my jobs from the college job board. I worked at various jobs like a bookkeeper, driver, janitor, cashier, stock clerk and receiving clerk. Yes my college career was going well.

My jobs were not overbearing. I was getting money. My financial aid was a great help also. Life was good except for one thing. I had to go home each day. My social life was still lacking. I had no girl. I spent a lot of lonely days and nights, lots of free social time with nothing to do. I had few friends at that time; a real basket case socially. As time moved forward into my second semester; school was still easy for me; and I loved it. I wasn't apprehensive anymore.

I had to pick elective courses. I became very creative when picking those classes. I remember taking a political science course. I excelled in that class. I was learning so much. My eyes began to be opened about some other things that were going on politically in the country. The teacher in my political science class was an African American woman that was very professional. I received a B+ in that class. As the semester rolled along, I was becoming more aware of the world around myself. The second year in school was when I stepped up to what I was really about. I started taking classes that really opened up my eyes. I took two African-American studies classes.

That really opened my eyes to the complexities of myself, and my skin color as it related to the rest of society. I received a dose of African-American history. I became attracted to it. All the self-loading and low self-esteem including all the negative thoughts I felt about myself started to subside a little bit. I ran with this knowledge. I received A's and B's in all my African-American studies classes. I soon changed my major. I wanted to be a college professor teaching African American history.

Yes I had new momentum. I studied into the early a.m. hours just about every night.

This extra studying, was not for class; was on my own, to further my own knowledge.

When black history month rolled around, there were always rallies and events. I always got on the agenda. People, who knew me from high school, could not believe their eyes. I had found my niche. I was kind of like Michael Jackson, in a sense that I was kind of a soft-spoken person; but I was fearless and hypnotic on stage. I felt the power. I was a political poet now. I was speaking along the lines of Gil—Scott, and the last poets. I was becoming huge in stature, and well known. I was finally getting a swagger for the first time in my life; when I wasn't on a basketball court. I was feeling better and better from the person who didn't fit in the black world or the white world. I now felt like I was blacker than the blackest black person. I was not talking about color. I was talking about having the knowledge of my history. I remember reading books like the Egyptian books and other books; including a book by Malcolm X. I studied Marcus Garvey, Martin R. Delaney, W.E.B. Dubois, Booker T. Washington and many others. I was filling my head with top notch black knowledge. I was jazzed to be running around the school with somewhat of a swagger. I was editor of my own newsletter. It was called Roots Aware. It stood for are we aware roots exist. There was a young lady who was a few years older than myself. She was more aware of life then I was at that time. She was my co-editor. I must give her credit. She was my friend.

My school life was going real well. I had mentors who were professors teaching black history; and I was enthusiastic.

I wasn't pure anymore either. I had met this lady of the night, one night that needed a ride to Oakland. I gave her a ride and also gave her what she was used to. I was still a rookie at the sex game, and I still felt like a rookie. I told my few friends that I had on the streets, who joked that I had gotten a two dollar prostitute. Yea, but nevertheless I was not pure anymore!

Nate at this time was unhappy that I was now a black history major. I'd come home and want to watch one of the few black shows that were on the TV at this time.

My father wondered why I was rolling with such new black thought, and new black excitement. He told me that black folks were never going to do a damn thing. I was shocked by that statement. I thought he would be proud of me. What it was was that from his experience, he had come to the conclusion that black people would never unite under our kinship. What he said inspired me to do a poll on the college campus. The theme was why black people don't unite. The results were fascinating. What I came to realize was that African American people as slaves, were brought from different countries in Africa. There were different tribes with a different foundation of customs and traditions. To get black people, 400 years later to unite around their skin color was not going to happen. I did read about Marcus Garvey and the Black Star line. He had millions of black people ready to go back to Africa. Black people had signed up. I believe as far as I remember reading that a few million were ready to go. The government took him on trumped up charges and deported him. Black people did establish a colony of people in Liberia. From what I understand though, it didn't work out so well. Therefore after that poll I realized that Nate was right. Black people were never going to fully unite on one common purpose; let alone on skin color. It started with me, at the beginning of my quest for history. I started off with a premise that I hated my dark skin. Although that was my feeling at the start; I began to be laced with historical information. I came upon the story of Willie Lynch.

I don't want to water down the story; and I do want to move forward about the warrior queen, but trying to keep it as simple as possible. The story as I understand it is that there was a master slave owner, I believe from the West Indies. I could be wrong about his original location. But at this point, who cares where he came from. Anyway he came by boat northward along the eastern part of the country. He was summoned by whatever means of communication available at that time. He came to what I believe was the east coast. He talked about being there to help the problems some of the people who owned slaves, were having with their slaves. He had a plan that he had been using. This plan he said, would not only handle the problem they were having with their slaves. He said he could solve their slave's problems for hundreds of years going forward. He told them he knew they were having problems because they summoned him, and also because he saw and smelled the hanging bodies of slaves along the way. He told them they have to pit the light-skinned blacks against the dark skin blacks. He said they had to pit the old blacks against the young blacks. They had to pit the women against the men. That's why you had the house Negroes who were closer to the master, played against the field Negroes. It's easy to understand that the field Negroes did not like the house Negroes, who did not have to work as hard as the field Negroes. The house Negroes felt superior to the field Negroes. There's no doubt that the house Negroes did not have to go through as much as the hard daily work, and the anger of the overseer. The house Negroes were also usually lighter in color then the field Negroes. Just like Willie Lynch said, separate them. To this day, it's the same way Willie Lynch predicted it. I felt it growing up, because of my dark skin. It was at that time I received the foundation of what was going on. Just like Willie Lynch said, "the slaves will be controlled for hundreds of years". Now here it is at the time of this writing, it's almost 2016, and it is the same as Willie Lynch said. Therefore I believe Nate was right. He may not have understood why, but from his experience he knew.

Then the next thing I discovered with my reading of black history was that your own people will be your own worst enemy as a potential black leader. Wow! I was learning enough to have a thin foundation of a black leader. Yet I know what I read. I knew that my own people will resist me, or possibly dislike me. But I continued to read, to study, to let myself be a student concerning my history. My speeches at black history celebrations grew more intense, more precise. Those were the time when rapping was really gaining a foothold in the black community. I knew I had the early foundation to be an excellent rapper. I just didn't have the musical background. I didn't have the street savvy. I didn't want to fake it. At that time business was no longer my major. It was definitely black history. I wanted to be a professor, teaching black history.

That's what I wanted to do with my life. I did know that I knew little about the streets. I knew it would be very difficult to reach the masses; because I didn't come from where they came from. I didn't grow up in the ghetto. All I knew about the problems of the masses I learned in a book. Little did I know that I would gain a full course education the hard way? What I learned in a book had nothing to do with the day-to-day grind of the ghetto. What I knew just wasn't the same. Yet it was because of the knowledge that gave me the chance I needed in life. I wanted to do something righteous with my life.

Things stayed the same for a number of months; the good and the bad. I was an excellent well-disciplined student. My social life was still suspect. I remember some Friday and Saturday nights I was looking out my window and wondering if I would ever get a mate. I wondered if my life would ever be fulfilled with a soulmate, a partner. Those were some very lonely days. As I was going to the second semester of the second year I had some sort of celebrity status on campus. I was the scholar I never was in high school. I was known now for my speeches at black history rallies. I was even elected a senator of the College of San Mateo associated students, student body. I was making a name for myself on the college campus. I was president of my own club. I was also a member of the black student union. Flying high at school was a constant. Yeah I still did my weed; but I never mixed weed and school. I was flying high on a natural high of academics; black history academics.

Sometime in 1983, I made a big mistake. There was a vice president who came to College of San Mateo. He came to give a speech. I thought this would be a great opportunity for me to ask him a question. There was a member of his cabinet that made a statement saying that America must continue to sever ties between Africans and African-Americans. I wanted to ask this vice president if he concurred with that statement. To tell the truth I wanted to embarrass him with that question. I showed up at the speech and walked in. I was wearing a bright orange African shirt. When I stepped in the room, I felt an eerie feeling. The room was packed. TV cameras, signs, and posters were everywhere. There were two lines on each side of the room. People were lining up for questions. I stepped to the left side, and got in line. There were three people ahead of me. On the right side there were four people in line. I felt like all eyes were on me. At that time I didn't think about it; but an African-American man, dressed in an orange African shirt, at a speech that a republican was giving. Yes the murmurs and whispers were about me. I was actually taking attention away from the speaker with my mere presence. They were allowing people to ask questions from the left side to the right side. When it was my turn to ask my question, question and answer period was over. I never got to ask my question; but it didn't matter. I was now a target, even though I didn't know it at that time.

The speech was on a Friday I believe. That previous Wednesday I had gotten hired to work at Bank of America. Remember readers this was 1981. At this time there was still talk about whether or not a black man had the mental capability to be a quarterback in the NFL. For me a black man to get hired at Bank of America in this climate was unusual. The fact that I was a square with good academics had gotten me into the door of a bank. After the speech on Friday, and throughout the weekend, I looked forward to my start date which was that Monday coming up.

I arrived at the bank dressed for work. The bank manager, the woman who hired me, approached with a stressful look on her face. She told me that she was very sorry.

She said this had never happened to her before. She said the corporate heads had disallowed my hiring. She was very apologetic, while continuing to tell me, that this had never happened before. I didn't understand it at the time. This had never happened to me before either. While writing this book I was able to look back and put the pieces together. Back then I never tied together the missed job opportunity with the mistake of walking into that speech. These people have too much power. Yet at the age of 20, I didn't have a clue what had happened. I didn't know it then. But I believe that I was a marked man. Something strange would happen again sometime later.

I first met Mary when she was a freshman. I was finishing up my second year. I had changed my major a couple of times, so I was going to have to come back the next year. I was so Afrocentric at that time. I met this young woman who had the same skin tone as mine. She wore a lot of cosmetics though. I think she had a little low self-esteem going on also. It was not my low self-esteem that held me back at that time. I befriended her. We would hang out on the grass as a lot of students did at school while doing our homework together. We had fun times together. My car situation at that time was back and forth. When I met her I didn't have my 1967 Chevy Malibu anymore. I believe I had a 1964 Chevy impala at that time. It was giving me lots of problems. I remember when it was time for her to get a car. I helped pick out an Audi fox. It really fit her. She worked at a bank. I remember she would let me drive that car while she was at work. I drove it all over while profiling. Just like guys will do. I was proud to have a mate. We were good friends before becoming lovers. And lovers we became. We would get hotel rooms all the time. Sex with her was plentiful and pleasurable. She was my friend and my lover. Finally my social life was showing some promise. I continued to live at home. Pops will forever have my gratitude for allowing me the chance to have a great foundation before leaving the nest. After some time I became complacent with Mary. I became disillusioned. I started taking for granted my life, my chance and broke up with Mary; she was a good woman. After some time, loneliness crept in again. I didn't know it, but I was setting myself up for or fall, for what was in front of me.

Nate was kind of a loner. He didn't stay in contact with his people very much.

Therefore we did not get a lot of family members visiting. They were few and far in between. His nephew, Nate's deceased sibling's son came to visit. I never met this man before. He was perhaps 30 or 32. He came from Los Angeles to visit Nate in the bay area; as part of this family vacation journey. He came in one night. I was introduced to him. I was very impressed with him. His demeanor, is confidence was what I wanted.

That man talked me into going to Los Angeles with him that night. I just left everything. I knew there was something I needed that I didn't have in San Mateo. He had the street cred. He had alfa man status. He had what I wanted.

Los Angeles was like walking into a foreign country to me. Everybody around me was hip, somewhat ghetto, sharper and faster than me. I had not lived that life. I came off as whitewashed and square; watered down even. My education was not a source of pride at that time; in the circles that I was in. I first moved to crawfish's house. He stayed in the city in LA that I don't remember; but he stayed with his mate and his mate's sibling. She was in her 30s; but she was all women. She looked kind of fine to me. His mate was out of town on her own vacation. I remember my young self with few clothes on, putting on a house coat. His mate's sibling was lying on the couch; asleep I thought. I lay down on the floor near the couch. I later found out she was not asleep. Yeah she told crawfish. I understand now that I acted like a immature nut. Crawfish told me "man, you got to talk to these women." I couldn't stay there anymore. He moved me to a relative of Teresa's side of the family. I stayed there for a of couple weeks at my relative Janet's house. She was actually the mate of a well-known deceased man's sibling. That man was a legendary, great Singer. I was now in his sibling's house. I did not know for years later that this man was the man! Janet's mate welcomed me with open arms. He handed me $20 and made me welcome. He said he was going out of town to do a job. He was a preacher, and he was a roofer. He made me comfortable, and made me feel like he was really going to take me under his wing. He was going to show me the ropes. So was Crawfish; but Crawfish was in his 30s and this guy was in his 50s. His name was Al. I knew I wasn't seasoned for the hip-hop culture I was now in. I waited for his return; but I didn't just sit and rest on my laurels. I went to the neighborhood college; called Southwest College. I went to the job board and pulled out job leads just like I did in the bay area.

Aunt Sarah lived in the Los Angeles area. Aunt Sarah was pretty poor. Her sons and daughters, my relatives, welcomed me into the household. I appreciated my kinfolk. I always had a problem remembering names. Therefore I began calling everybody cuz. That was the wrong thing to say in that area. I had no idea about the crips and the bloods ordeal. The crips I believe were also called cuz. That's okay, except for the fact that I was in the blood area.

I remember walking, looking for a job because that was me. I walked very long distances; and found something that I had never seen. I saw signs in windows, offices, storefronts and warehouses that said no help wanted. I had never seen that before. I was invited to parties by Crawfish and other relatives. But I wasn't ready for that. I stayed there maybe three or four weeks. I didn't like it there. And I didn't fit in there. I felt like a foreigner. Just because I had black skin didn't matter. I was way over my head in the ghetto. I did a painting job from Crawfish. I got the money, and used it to purchase a bus ticket back to the bay. I managed to stay away from danger but that was not my speed. Actually it was much faster than me. The one thing I did do was have a good intimate experience. That was it.

Upon getting back to the bay area, back to San Mateo, I felt at home. But something had changed in me. I hooked back up with Mary, and began to live my young life. I felt a little more seasoned; but I really wasn't. I had just gotten a little more experience of what black life was like unsheltered. I was a very fortunate young man. Although now I wasn't the idealistic young man I used to be. The black history in me started to subside. I didn't want to be a black leader anymore. I didn't really know if I wanted to be a black history major anymore either. My life was now rudderless. Mary began to notice that my values were slowly changing. I wasn't talking much black thought. My thoughts and words were more like other people trying to get what they didn't have.

If I could have transferred myself 20 years later, the warrior queen would have laughed at me. I was not thinking good thoughts. I was now thinking get over thoughts.

I read about the atrocities perpetrated against my people, black people. I didn't dislike white people, not at all. I did not like what was done to my people. I moved back in the middle of the school semester; therefore going back to school immediately was not an option. I needed to work; to make some money. I found a job. At that time in the bay jobs were plentiful. I started working, but my thoughts were about having fun. The jealousy I had always had of the streets, players and hustlers was intense.

I remember I had purchased an old Cadillac for $100. The car was an old convertible boat,it smelled . But that car ran great. I ended up wrecking that car; horse playing. It still ran good, but there was an ugly, major mass of metal, dent in the front of the car. I still drove around in that car. There was no driver's window. I taped a piece of clear plastic to the inside driver's door, to cover the window that was missing. I didn't call it a Cadillac anymore. Those days were over. I hung out at the King rec center.

The same place I used to work at daily. I would sit in my car, watched the people go in and out, and smoke my weed; after playing basketball.

One day a guy walked up to me that I knew was a nut. Everybody had always labeled him as a nut. His name was Darren. Darren came up to the car and told me he would give me $20 cash and put $20 in my gas tank, to take him to San Jose; which was about 40 miles away. I told him to get in. I began to drive and he told me that he had some credit cards that were not his. When we got to the gas station he went inside to pay for the gas. I took one of his credit cards from him and slipped it into my shirt pocket. We drove to San Jose and while I was driving to the place he wanted to go, law enforcement got behind me, and put the lights on me. I pulled over. He asked if anybody in the car was on parole or probation. I said "no, I've never been detained". He asked Darren. Darren told him that he was on parole. He said "everybody out the car". We were searched and cuffed. He found the bag of credit cards and asked who they belonged to. We both said "not mine." It wasn't until I had the cuffs on me when I realized that I had that credit card in my pocket. I was devastated, feeling pretty stupid. I was going to get locked up, now no longer a scholar. Now I was going to be a detained. I initially didn't stay in their very long. I was released in a couple of days after going to court; and given a court date with instructions to return. I fully intended to come back. I had no car now. I was just happy to be free. I caught the bus back home and lived until the court date. I was ready. I had my mate, who was ready to take me to San Jose, Santa Clara County, to make my court appearance. I called her to come get me. She said her car wouldn't start. I ran over to her house; and sure enough the car didn't start. I called the courthouse to tell them the truth; with my naïve self. The truth was that the car wouldn't start and I would not be able to make it. The next thing I noticed I had a bench warrant.

Teresa said that two cops had come to the door looking for me. I then ran the streets.

I obviously couldn't go home. I was no street person; but I now started living like a fugitive, living house to house. I would go to the neighborhood hole in the wall club and have fun. There was an older woman that took a liking to me and let me stay at her house briefly. That was briefly, because her old man was getting freed and coming home. I stayed at a house that me and a so-called friend of mine broke into.

Actually it was a house that we knew the people had been busted; and we knew that no one was there. I cooked eggs, potatoes and there was some bacon there too. My friend looked out the window and said he saw law enforcement. I took my license out and stuck it under some furniture; just in case I got caught. I figured at least they would not know who I was. I was real naïve then. They never came in the house. And we both left. I went back to Teresa's house to at least sleep the night. I began to ponder my next move and try to get some sleep. Sleep didn't come that quickly though. I suddenly remembered that I had left my license underneath that furniture. I had to go back over there around 2 AM, and bust back in to get my ID; unbelievable! I was not cut out to be a fugitive. The next day I told Teresa goodbye; and made the long bus ride to San Jose. I knew little about the criminal justice system. I had gotten the dui once; and that was one of my few dances with the criminal justice system. I didn't know that I had a chance to put myself on the calendar to go back to court. I just needed to turn myself in.

Besides the dui, and this situation, the only experience I had with the law was way back when I was about 19. Arnold and I went over to my friend's house, to play a game back then called intellivision. It was the early version of today's ps1, 2 and 3s. Arnold took this TV over there, so we could play on a good TV. We all drank, and I drank a little too much. It was okay because I was still aware. I was just too juiced to drive. It was okay because I wasn't driving. I came with my friend. He proceeded to drive me home with Arnold driving behind. He had a accident. He got locked up.

Now I was getting locked up. It seemed like it took forever to process me. After all there was no rush for them. I wasn't going anywhere, anytime soon.

From scrub in high school, to a scholar in college, to incarceration, that's what was happening. That's what the transition was. I wasn't focused too much on my past life, at that time. I was getting a dose of real life behind bars. Yeah it wasn't the penitentiary like Mark had been in. It was just like the penitentiary to me at that time. After taking what it seemed like forever processing me; I finally got into my cell. It was a two man pod that let me into the general area for meals. I was an unsentenced felon; and didn't have any clue when I was getting out. My cellmate was about my age; maybe a little older. I never really had any run ins; except one time. One day during lunch I did not eat a sandwich.

I hid it to eat later in my cell. That was against the rules. I wasn't a bad guy; but I wanted to do what I wanted to do over that small matter. My roommate took offense that I didn't offer him any. Either it was some protocol, or he was just trying to play me; to try me. I threw the sandwich away. I thought why I should share something with him, when he had gotten the same sandwich. That was not going to happen. Anyway I followed protocol for the most part after that. I wasn't trying to make any waves. So here I was this square guy, in a non-square situation. I was a little apprehensive; but not scared. Scared was not at all on the agenda. Scared would have gotten me negative focus. People in there fed on scared like a plague. I just blended in with the majority. It was the thing to do. I stayed in maximum security for about three weeks; until I heard my name called "Solomon! roll em up." That meant role my bedding, mattress, towels, toothpaste, and everything I had in there. I was going elsewhere. I grabbed everything; and I walked in my orange jumpsuit, that was too long for me. I walked to the door. The guards buzzed me through to another door that I went through. I was escorted with others to another area of the facility. I was going to medium security.

I had turned myself in, in San Jose; which is in Santa Clara County. I was driven to Milpitas California; which I believe is east of San Jose. That is where they housed those who were going to be staying there for a while. San Jose is a great city. I lived there a few years later, for a brief period of time. Santa Clara County, which houses San Jose is a great place; as long as you stay on the right side of the law. If a person is trying to do wrong, Santa Clara County is not the place. You will get caught up.

They don't play there. So now I was headed to medium security.

Medium security was a little better. I gave up my orange jumpsuit for different attire. I don't remember what it was, but it wasn't orange anymore. Medium security was different, with the respect that there were no man pods; that let out to the general population. I was among the general population. It was loud. The TV was always on some lower-level kids type programs; cartoons and lower education type stuff. I managed to endure, to adjust.

In the medium security one did eat better. That was the first thing I noticed. I was in court like once every 3 to 4 weeks. I didn't comprehend the end game too much. It was just a lot of legal mumbo-jumbo to me. I developed a routine. I did a lot of reading. I stayed there for perhaps 4 to 5 weeks before hearing my name called again "Solomon! Roll em up." That's the sound every man wanted to hear. Yet I wasn't going home that day. I was going to minimum security.

Minimum-security was just like it sounds, the security was minimum. I got to go out on the grounds, which of course was surrounded by a barbed wire fence. Yet there was a baseball field. I played a little baseball. I hit a couple shots down the third base line; keeping the person on third base on his toes. I caught a ball hit to me in right field. I tried to throw the runner out; tagging from third base, but I never had a strong arm, he scored.

I got to walk from dorm to dorm. There were always either cartoons or music videos on each and every TV, in each dorm. There were pretty birds everywhere. We were told that another year will be added to our sentences; if we harmed one of the birds.

I never received any correspondence from the outside world. I knew none of my siblings would write me. They were too busy with their own lives. Moms and pops were not going to write me either. I didn't have a problem with my family not writing me. I was very disappointed that Mary didn't write.

Mary was very watchful and careful of the stigma of having her mate in jail. She didn't even want to live with any guy at this time. She thought it was so typical of black people; and she didn't want that. Mary also didn't want a child without marriage. She thought that to be typical. I was now in behind bars, even though she knew that that wasn't my nature. She never wrote me back when I wrote her. Yeah I was really hurt by that. I waited and waited after writing her. Her letter never came. Out of anger I wrote her sibling after almost 3 months in the hoosegow. I wrote her sibling out of spite; because Mary would not write me. I wrote her sibling also because she was classy, fine and had a Coke bottle shape. I was done with Mary for not writing me back. Her sibling did write me back; with the turndown of course. I did appreciate her taking the time. I had no money on my books at that time. When commissary time came around I had no money to buy anything; outside of what was provided for me. I came up with a plan to make money.

These guys around me were mostly of a lower educational level. I played on that. They had mates. Some of them had seemed to lose some of their game. I was a poet. I would ask guys to tell me something about the girl. If it was a birthday or special holiday or something, I would get information about their girl; whatever they wanted to say and put it in a poem. I would include their girl's name in it; and make it rhyme and shine. I would even draw a little cartoon. I was real good as an artist and a poet. I would charge five dollars each. I was starting to rack up money from the so called players, hustlers and criminals. No, low self-esteem was not shown in there. Low self-esteem D.L. was working these thugs, misfits and players out of money because of my education, talent and art mastery.

I did take a few unnecessary chances. I remember purchasing some weed. The tiniest one I ever smoked in my life, for five dollars. That was real intense. I basically had to finish it up in two or three inhales, because getting caught in there with weed, or even under the influence of weed was some real serious time. I finished up quickly. I never got caught, which was real fortunate for me.

After about 84 days inside. I got a court date, and was told that I would be released. I did get released after 92 days. I was released at about 12 midnight in Milpitas. There were no buses running to take me into San Jose. I walked for about three hours. I got to San Jose and had to wait another 2 to 3 hours for buses to start running. I had to go to Santa Clara County into San Mateo County. I went from city to city until I got to San Mateo. I thought and felt like that life was over. For the most part it was. I did meet Johnny Law more times in my life; but those times were minimal. I was happy to be free.

When I got back home things had moved on, and changed. Arnold was now living in my room. Aunt Laura was staying there now. She and Nate were working together. Pops would get jobs remodeling old houses and hauling. Man did that man work, constantly. As time passed I had to get myself going on something. School was not an immediate option for me. I needed cash. Yeah I found a job. I always did in the bay. I shined in the interviews. I worked until I had enough money to purchase a car. I continued to work and hang out at night. I really had no plan for my life at this point. I just knew I had to maintain and hold my own. Once again I appreciate my pops for allowing me the opportunity to get myself together while he continued to pay the bills in the house.

CHAPTER 3

The transition! Came as quite a surprise!

AROUND THIS TIME, I guess Pops was making moves like he always said he would.

Arnold had moved out. Pops said he was losing the house. I don't know, I will never really know the real reason; for pops could not afford to pay the note anymore. Maybe it was intentional. I will never really know. Moms was moving to her sibling's house in Menlo Park California. Menlo Park was perhaps 20 miles to the south of San Mateo. Menlo Park set right next door to East Palo Alto; which was kind of a ghetto at that point. Menlo Park was sandwiched between East Palo Alto, Palo Alto and Atherton. Atherton housed lots of rich people; celebrities and athletes. Menlo was also close to Palo Alto which was filthy rich. This was part of the time Bill Gates and Steve Jobs were there doing their thing in garages; or wherever they started. This time was before the dawn of the term Silicon Valley.

Anyway, moms moved to her sibling's house in Menlo Park. Arnold got a job at the St. Matthews Hotel; in downtown San Mateo. I at this time had little choice. I also moved to Menlo and stayed with James. His name was James J Johnson Jr. I say his full name because he's deceased now. This man was one-of-a-kind. He was a retired construction worker; who also worked on the San Mateo Bridge. He would tell you quickly "I got mine soul, you get yours". He called himself, cool papa, cool breeze. He would say things like "pop your toes, goodness knows, say it loud, I'm black and I'm proud, ha ha, black and can't help it. He was a real proud man. He was proud of his accomplishments. He was also a real ego maniac.

Pops was still in San Mateo; living with Aunt Laura. I got a job in Menlo. I worked 12 hours a day and six days a week. This was the most money to that point I had had in my life.

After taxes I was bringing home over $500 a week. I just didn't have much time to spend my money. When I did spend, I wasn't spending wisely. I was pretty lonely for a female.

Around New Year's in the early 80s I purchased a suit. It was a five piece suit. I went to Sacramento California. I just wanted to get out of town and meet someone. I had a pocket full of money and I was dressed clean. I got off the bus and got a hotel room. I got in a cab and told him to take me where the happening spot was. When he dropped me off I went inside the club. It was jumping. I was not a good dancer; but I did what I did. A pretty fine young lady that I had danced with took notice of me. When the club was closing she approached me. I went home with her. She let me explore every hole her body had to offer. To put it plaining, it was a real good intimate experience. I don't remember her name. I do remember that she had two sons. What she wanted was someone to help raise her off-spring. Her sons were about nine and 10. They seem to be great kids; but me moving to sac town, aka Sacramento; quitting my job, didn't seem like the thing to do for me at that time in my life. I felt I was way too young to take on that set of responsibilities. She told me that if I was interested, send her some money; otherwise she was moving on. Life was hard for her; and she needed help with her sons. I don't remember asking her what happened; to her mate or mates; but I assumed incarceration could have been a reason. We moved on and lost contact.

I ended up losing my job. I also moved out of James's house. I moved back to San Mateo; and stayed at the St. Matthews Hotel. Oh yeah, I forgot to mention that one of those $500 checks I had, I ran into some scrubs. I got stuck and smoked almost $500 worth of substance, with help, for the first time. I was stuck like chuck; as the saying goes. They played me like a fiddle. I forgot about that. I thought it was just something that happened that day; and would never happen again. Wow was I in for a reality check.

Chapter 4

I became a substance abuser

I SECURED A JOB at a company in San Carlos California. San Carlo is about halfway between San Mateo and Menlo Park; actually closer to San Mateo to the south. This company was like one of the first major corporations I worked for. I was a stock clerk. I actually liked my job at the beginning. I counted parts to put into kits. Anything I did that included counting was all right with me. I was 23 years old at this point in my life. I had my own place. I stayed at the hotel; but it suited my needs at that point in my life. I had a room. There was a shared bathroom down the hall. I only brought home about $235 per week. I stayed pretty low-key. I pretty much just went to work, came home and smoked my weed in the evenings. I was only an occasional drinker. My life was pretty simple until I decided to complicate it.

I saw him when he checked into the hotel. He was a flashy dresser; and the woman on his arm was hot. He checked into a room on the third floor. I was on the second floor. I saw him go in and out of the hotel. He always seemed to have a new girl under his arm. Arnold worked and stayed at the hotel. He told me one day, that someone he knew was looking for someone, to sell some weed. As I look back now, Arnold and weed, here I go again. Yeah I was a grown man, responsible for making my own decisions. I met the guy, and began buying weed from him. It was some lower-level weed; that he didn't charge me much for. I started selling the weed and was flipping it pretty good. I was smoking for free; and smoking a lot of it. I was still going to work every day. I wasn't messing that up.

One day he approached me, talking about Mr. clean, with the multiple women. He wanted to buy some weed. He wanted to get it on credit. Normally I wouldn't do that; but I did this time. It was a disaster. He said he would pay me next Tuesday. He said he had no money then. For the next two weeks, I still got no money out of him. I was thinking of things to do to him now. I confronted him again. He told me to come to his room on Wednesday. Wednesday came around and I approached his room consciously. I didn't know what to expect; but it was about respect. Just like those three thugs years earlier; it was about respect. I knocked on the door. He opened the door and motioned for me to come in. I came in and sat down. There was a glass table in the middle of the floor. This glass table had all kinds of pipes, glass pipes and all types of stuff that was not too recognizable to me.

He handed me a package that I opened. It looked like powder. Yeah I had snorted powder before. I always saw it as a rich man's thing. It was not a part of what I did. I took the package as payment. I figured he owed me $25 for the weed. He handed me $25 worth of powder. I took it like we were even. I got up to leave. He asked me to sit down; and then he proceeded to smoke some with me. At that moment I didn't even tie into months earlier when I smoked up almost $500 with help of course. I smoked some and I wasn't immediately snared like some other people would tell me later. I got up to leave; and actually purchased some already rocked up powder for other purposes.

I took the powder that I would later learn to turn powder into rock. I took the powder and the rock downstairs to my room. I did no more that night. The next day I put my plan into action. This time was in the early 1980s. Powder had always been around; but now rock was the best kept secret. Women were going crazy for it.

And that was my plan; to get women by using the rock as the lure. I knew there was at least one young woman at the plant that had a history for doing whatever one wanted her to do for the rock.

I had an additional duty in addition to being a stock clerk. I was also the smock man. I had to go all over the plant, and collect people's dirty smocks. I had to replace the dirty smocks, with clean ones. It was a job no one in the stock area wanted. The job was given to the last man hired. I turned a negative into a positive. It allowed me the freedom to go all over the plant; and see if I could get my mack on. I pulled up in Veras area. I had not even met her properly. I had the rock in my hand. I moved past her. I just opened my hand and closed it quickly. I just wanted to show her that I had the rock. I saw her eyes light up and I left. It's funny; I don't remember ever leaving the plant and seeing her. I saw her this day, and talked her into coming with me.

I didn't have a car at this time. We caught two buses to get to my hotel. I stopped at the liquor store down the street from my hotel. I bought some wine, zigzags, a pipe with screens, matches and a hero sandwich. I never liked going back to get anything. So I made sure I had everything in front of me. I wanted to be self-sufficient. Oh yeah I picked up some protection too. I wanted to get busy with her. She of course, wanted to smoke first. I gave her a little taste of the pipe; but hey, I wanted to get busy. She was too interested in the glass pipe. I finally put myself inside of her. She knew what was up.

She knew what we were there for. I finished my business with her that night. She finished the rock which I was not too much into at that point. I just knew I had a good way to get some girls now. Vera went home, and I laid down thinking about my next conquest.

I pushed my smock car throughout the plant; looking for new conquests. I got together with a woman named Regina.

We decided to get a place together. I was starting to do a little rock now weekly. A month earlier I had smoked up my rent money for the week; for the hotel. I thought that was just a one-time thing; but it was just the beginning.

Her Old Lady found us a nice little place in in East Palo Alto; a one-bedroom apartment.

It set along the frontage road of the 101 freeway. It was cool, except for the fact that I was now living in a city named East Palo Alto. We were an up and coming couple.

Both of us worked at the same company. We loved each other. We were both 23 and 24. It was an exciting beginning. We got paid weekly; so I still did my weekly splurges with the rock. It got to be very hard to keep it at the $25 per week limit. I was getting stressed about the living situation. My freedom was gone. My spending on the rock surpassed $25 per week. I was not happy in this current situation. I didn't know how to talk to her about the situation. It just seemed easier to smoke some more. At this time she didn't know about my splurges with the rock.

She was not lacking in confidence and definitely spoke her mind. On the contrary was me. I was more of a laidback person. It was kind of a turnoff to me; the fact that she was so vocal. I even started working on another shift so that I could have some separation. All that did was given me more time to smoke. My smoking speeded up to more than once a week.

Eventually she found out about it; because I couldn't keep up with my obligations. I then thought, by selling it I would be able to stay even. That situation never got off the ground though. I mixed some dope up, and put so much cut in it that someone would have come back and wanted to do me harm; after seeing what they bought from me.

Things just got worse and worse. I turned to God, and started going to church. The preacher found out that we were sharing the same address; and started putting pressure on us to marry. I took the bait.

We got married. Her Old Man paid for everything. He didn't know his daughter was marrying a substance abuser. Yes that's what I was becoming fast. I was way over my head. I was overwhelmed and unhappy.

She went on a trip to Mississippi. I had women in the house, although I didn't cheat on her. It did look like I cheated on her though. Now I was feeling like a chump. I was feeling pretty low waiting for her to return and find out what I done.

I was in the bathroom when I heard her scream. I knew at that second that it was over. I had failed her and myself. I had failed miserably. I moved to Teresa's house; that I had previously helped get her own place, perhaps 15 minutes away.

This was the beginning of what was to become 13 years of madness. I was no he man hero. I was still overweight. I knew little about life. I ran on the stability of the teaching I had growing up. Be kind, considerate, provider, respectful to women; etc, etc, etc; all goods traits; Inside of myself, though I was an emotional wreck. That was a breeding ground for my future issues. We lived together a little over two years. We were only married for seven months. I purposely omitted all the irresponsible actions I did while in this relationship; while in this marriage.

This book is centered on my 17 years married to the warrior queen. I just wanted to give some background of where I came from. My actions, my history and where I came from.

What obstacles I overcame to be in position, to be the man to the warrior queen.

I do have another book that's coming out after this one. It will be called "Looking back through the crack, from crack fiend to millionaire, God let him live".

Therefore I will leave the history of my greater issues to the pages of my other book. Also to my memory and memories of others who had to live through my, immaturity and devastation.

I will mention that during the marriage I did go through one program. It was a 30 day spin-dry at a facility. The insurance from the job paid for it. They paid about $12,000. I did smoke weed two weeks into the stay. When I got out I smoked the very next day. I saw my mate's sibling. We used to use together. All that program talk went out of my head immediately. I had $10 in my pocket that day. I disappeared quick with him, and used.

A year later my marriage was over. I was staying at Teresa's house; still in East Palo Alto, now in full-blown using mode. I tried to get back in the facility I was in a year earlier. Yet I was three days too late. The insurance coverage was only good for one year later. Not a year and three days.

It was 1986 now. I was 25 years old and had little grip on reality. Substance was too easy to get in that city. I don't care if I had one dollar, two dollars, it didn't matter. I could get it right across the street; or even next door.

Right across the street, at the liquor store, at this time, there could possibly be 20 to 30 dealers in open competition, waiting for you when you walked out the store; or soliciting you as you came in. The strange thing was that the law building was right across the street. Upon reflection, looking back, I was told that the law was selling substances; through the teenagers; who were controlling the game in East Palo Alto.

I finally left Teresa's house and entered a long-term rehab facility in San Jose. It was a year program. I have nothing but good things to say about that program. Even though they kicked me out after about 10 months.

It was a huge house with six or seven rooms. There were about four residents per room. This was a male and female facility. The cultures were mixed.

They financially operated by getting people on the county general assistance so they could get paid. They also operated on donations and fundraising. The residents participated by having car washes. Regardless, the facility stayed afloat.

It was a tough, thorough program. We were not allowed to go anywhere without someone escorting us for the first three months. Someone had to have much more clean time than you had; to escort you to court. Appointments like medical or wherever one had to go;

one had support. There were briefings and debriefings. When you left the facility, you were told to go directly to the appointment with no deviation. You were briefed and debriefed when you returned.

You had to tell wherever you went step-by-step. It was a good discipline because substance abusers are very smart, crafty individuals. They are capable of manipulating anyone to get high.

1986 turned into 1987. I even received a letter in the mail from Regina. It was the finalization of our parting ways. Even though we had not been together for over a year; it still hurt me and brought tears to my eyes that I let her down. I put her through a lot of pain and embarrassment. I was very sorry for that. I was just trying to get myself better now. I couldn't undo the past.

As the months moved forward, I was turning into a senior resident. I was learning how to stay sober. It was a very clean and sober environment. I thought I was a pretty good role model resident. One day after I had been in the year program for about 9 1/2 months, I was asked to escort a fairly new resident to a court appearance in Redwood City; which was in San Mateo County; my neck of the woods. I accepted the assignment of course; like I had a choice. We were briefed and told to go exactly where we were supposed to go. We were supposed to go to the court and back. We were given bus tickets and clear direction. We were told not to deviate from our destination. We were told not to talk to any loaded people. We let them know that we understood. We went on our way. That was the plan, and we set out to do what was in front of us. We went forward through Santa Clara County and into San Mateo County. I think we had to take four buses each way. We went to court and were on our way back. It was a very hot day. It was unusually hot that day in Redwood City. I asked Jerry if he wanted something to drink. He said yes and I told him that we were not supposed to do this. Nevertheless we went to a store where I purchased sodas for him and myself. We finished the store run and headed for the bus stop. We caught all the buses and headed back to the facility. We were debriefed. We were asked if we went to our destination. We said yes. We were asked if we talked to any loaded people. We said no. We were asked if we deviated. We said no. That was not the truth.. I thought nothing of it. We didn't use anything. But that was part of the untruth that got me kicked out of the house.

That soda I got. The deviation to the store was classified as deviating, even though the store was right across the street from the bus stop.

The leaders of the facility could tell something was going on in the house. A lot of these people were former users. There was something going on in the house. Either that or they were just squeezing us because they could.

They put the whole house, perhaps 27 people, women and man in a group; in a circle. I was now a senior resident. They said something was going on. They said there are secrets that need to be told. They told us that we were going to sit in a circle until somebody gave it up. I certainly had no secrets to tell. We sat there for 45 minutes. Nobody gave up anything. Until all of a sudden Jerry stood up and told them that when he and I went to court last week we deviated and went to the store. I melted in my seat. I was a senior resident. I was put out the program for that reason.

I now had 10 months clean and sober under my belt; so I figured I was ready to live life now. I guess it was about 1987 now. I was about 26 years old. A young man ready to live life again, I was given two weeks to find a job and a place to stay.

I went out each day looking and found a job. I moved initially into a hotel and looked forward to living my life at that time, sober; yeah so I thought.

I stayed in the hotel for about three weeks. I liked my job. I was a stock clerk again. I liked using my mind especially with numbers. The job was going well. I was stacking money. I was not going to any meetings though. No 12 step meetings, no church; just work and back home. I was optimistic about my future. I wanted to find a new place to stay; and eventually a car.

One of my coworkers, a black man, who looked like Sinbad the comedian, told me he had a room for rent. The price he was going to charge me was actually lower than the hotel. He was about 10 years older than I was. He had a good lease on life. He was married and they had property. He became like a mentor to me for a while. I stayed there a little less than a month.

One day Arnold and I were talking on the phone. He was going to sell his car. I had already been disappointed earlier the last week. An ex-employer was selling a van and I was very interested. When I got to check it out, it wasn't what I expected. Disappointed, yes but now I was trying to buy Arnold's car. He said he had to leave by 4 pm. It was 2 pm then. So I had to get to East Palo Alto; with $800 to buy this car. I also had 11 and half months clean and sober. My $800 took 3 days to leave me; but my sobriety left that day. Yeah I was devastated. To make matters worse I was running around with an ugly woman. She was trying to clip me, hustle me, and play me all along. She didn't get a chance until the end.

But still, I was now broke, out of a job, and the guy I was renting a place from, dropped off all my stuff at my Teresa's house in East Palo Alto. So after a year I was right back where I started. My second program didn't work; because I did not continue to do what I was trained to do outside of the program.

I ran around East Palo Alto doing the same petty hustle I was doing a year earlier. I'm purposely not mentioning much of the nitty-gritty details about what went on in a lot of my habit days because the book is not about that..

Obviously I was not even close to be able to step to the warrior queen at that time. I continued to do lower-level hustles to get my substance at that time. While living at Teresa's house. I stayed there for about six months. I had had enough. I think she had had enough of seeing me in that life. I went back to San Jose and managed to get into another program. It was a year program at the San Jose rescue mission.

It was another year program. The year was 1989. I was 28 years old then.

Once again I was a model resident at the mission. Everybody had a job in the facility. I elevated myself to positions of cook and also night guard. Both positions guaranteed one with his own room with a TV. It of course was a religious-based program. One was in the program at the Mission; but helping the homeless daily was the real therapy. Seeing the homeless come in and out daily was a very humbling experience. After about six months I was even allowed to go to one of the neighboring cities junior college. I went to De Anza College in Cupertino. I had great hopes and dreams that I would be able to rekindle my education and actually finish school when I got out the program.

At the time of this writing January 2016 I really can't remember why I left the mission. I do remember the greatest earthquake that I've been through in 1989, the earthquake where the bridge fell down. I was in the kitchen cooking at the mission for the homeless. I cooked five meals a day. Two meals were cooked for the residents, and two meals were cooked for the homeless. The last meal of the day was cooked for the homeless and the residents combined.

I saw the ground roll just like the little things that move your car along at the car wash. The ground inside the dining room was moving like waves. I couldn't believe it. I had been in maybe three or four earthquakes that I can remember, since I was a kid growing up in the Bay Area; but they were nothing like this.

I moved back to East Palo Alto; mom's house again. I was soon doing some of the same behavior after about a month. Finding a job was a little difficult. My patience ran out. I worked a few temporary jobs; got my check and never returned.

I did notice after I started using again; that my hustle was getting better. It had to; I was a basket case. I would walk from East Palo Alto; walk down one long street, to Palo Alto, to hustle some money for my get high. I got better and better at talking people out of their money. I would tell people a sad luck story; using big college words. Most people believed me because of my vocabulary. My gut wrenching fabrications and my easy-going demeanor also gave me success. I became very good at doing something very bad. I was gaining hundreds of dollars; which was all going in the pipe.

My mom was getting sicker. Bernice came down from Stockton; and talked her into getting medical help. Moms ended up getting both legs removed. She ended up having to go into a care facility.

But she also talked me into going to Stockton with her. She was a counselor at a facility there. I went with her headed to my fourth program.

As Teresa was admitted to a care facility, Bernice set her sights upon me. Yes she talked me into going to Stockton with her. At first glance she was a teacher, teaching the bible; but she had graduated that program at the Stockton mission with a degree.

I entered the mission the first day, and I was showed around. Yeah it was old; a lot older than the mission in San Jose. I managed to navigate myself to a job in the kitchen. I guess good cooks are hard to find. Therefore that was my first job. Church service was held about three or four times a day.

It was a much more rigorous schedule. There were no TVs in the main mission. One read the Bible and read it a lot, they were speaking in tongues. That was the first time I experienced someone speaking in tongues and then someone interpreting. Of course each day the urge to get high was less and less intense. I read and read. I got a real good close relationship with God.

I was trying to connect my new relationship with God with the rules and regulations of the mission. It became harder and harder to do. There was a women and family mission next door. Contact with the women that came over to the main mission several times a day, to have service was forbidden.

I did thrive in my reading and my spirituality. There was a test given to determine what level one was going to be at while we were preparing to go to Bible College. I was the valedictorian of the test. I scored the highest of everyone. It seems that education that caused so much ill will from the street crowd was now an asset for me; and would be much later in my life. I was happy that I scored so high. I was also happy Bernice was proud of me. She had gone through the same testing process; and she graduated with a bachelor's degree.

I went forward, one month, two months; I made a few friends in there. I also met a young lady from the lady's shelter, briefly. I wanted to contact her. She was a fine figure of a woman. I switched my job from cook to driver. I was now a driver that was coached by an older man who had been doing that for decades. I had a driver's license and was ready. I was shown routes to missions in Tracy, Modesto etc. We went just about everywhere picking up donations. We also delivered mail from time to time. I found out the address of the mission next door; and slipped in a letter from myself to the woman at the shelter next door. She responded back by letter.

Therefore the no contact rule was being broken by both of us. I was very happy to get letters from her. She in turn enjoyed my correspondence. My stock was rising at the mission. There was also a young woman that worked in the kitchen that took a liking to me. I liked her for that friend, but didn't see a future especially because she had 3 to 4 teeth missing in front of her mouth. I couldn't hang with that.

One day the women and shelter couples set to have service as usual. This day was different in the respect that the topic centered on Jezebel and the Bible.

The woman I was corresponding with became very agitated and ran out on the service area. They were really laying it on thick. It seemed like the whole service was centered on discrediting her. I found out later that a letter I had written was found by one of the staff. They put a lot of pressure on her.

It seems she had a history. I guess she had been there at the mission before; and got involved in some level with a married man. They really gave her the blues for that. The way they did her really upset me. I was pretty angry they did her like that.

At this time I wanted to believe in the speaking in tongues. I prayed that night, and I asked God if that was really him speaking through the people. I asked God to speak to me the next day. I asked him to let me know if I should stay there. The next day during service someone spoke up and spoke in tongues. Someone else stood up and interpreted what was said. What the interpreter said was "I have given you a foundation. Go out to the highways and byways and spread my word. Go out to the highways and byways and spread my word" I went upstairs after the service and started packing my clothes. The residents asked me what I was doing. So I told them that the Lord said it was time to go. Someone told me that the Lord did not tell me that. They told me that the devil told me that. No one could tell me anything. I had prayed, asked and received my answer. I kept packing although I knew that I didn't have the money for the bus, for the two hours journey back to the bay.

At the moment, I did not care because I knew the Lord was going to provide a way. I got I believe $40 from a young man nicknamed legs because he was a double amputee, who I had befriended. I told Bernice I was leaving, and she was not happy about it.

I made my way to the bus station and waited for the bus to San Jose; because I knew there were men's shelters there at that time.

My sister was not happy that I left because she knew that was probably the last time I would see her. She had acquired the AIDS virus some years before. She was taking medicine for her illness; but had not told me she was sick. Her husband convinced her not to tell me; because they knew I would stay there for that reason alone. It turned out she got that virus from either sexual relations with her husband or sharing a needle with him. I really don't know for sure how or why, she acquired the virus. But they were using together. I'm not completely sure how it happened but I know he passed away first. She passed away sometime later in 1994 at this time it was the early 1990s. I was 29 years old and thought I had gotten my life on track.

There were a few men shelters in San Jose at that time. I knew my way around.

And I took advantage. I got off the bus, and took a light rail; basically a kind of half bus, half train that ran daily. It took me close to the shelter. I stood in line would all my bags, and checked into the shelter. Basically the simple rules were that one had to check in by 6 pm each day in order to keep their bed. One was responsible for one chore; either in the morning or the evening. There was one small bed divided by partitions for one's privacy. There was one TV on in the evenings. I slept well that night.

With my fourth program under my belt and a renewed closeness with God; I was ready, so I thought. I left the shelter the next day; going about acquiring maps and numbers. I signed up with a school and entered the culinary arts program. I thought it was a good foundational move. I always enjoyed cooking and was looking for a long-term job. As the day went by, I liked the school and was really digging in; in order to gain traction and talent. The problem that arose was that I needed money to acquire cooking clothes. I needed to find a job. I went to school five days a week; and also looked for work. After four or five days I had found a job.

It was a little unconventional, but it was a job. I became an ice cream man. I needed special clearance from the shelter to be able to come in later than 6 PM. Now I was acquiring knowledge that I was learning and developing. I also had some cash flow now. I was pretty happy now. I learned the ice cream game quickly. After school I would catch the bus to the ice cream yard. I would check in with the bosses. They rented out the ice cream trucks. The bill had to be paid weekly. We also bought the ice cream from them. I loved it. Therefore each week I would settle my account; by paying my ice cream bill. Then I would stock my truck with new ice cream. Whatever I was short of I would order. I would restock gas up and be out. I loved the freedom.

I did not limit myself with the route I was given. It was a route that situated in San Jose. It was cool, but I knew San Mateo County. Therefore that's where I started selling. I gassed up my truck and rolled over 40 miles to San Mateo County. I hit the best spots in every city. From East Palo Alto, Palo Alto, Menlo Park, Redwood City, San Carlos, San Mateo, Burlingame, Millbrae and San Bruno, I was making real good money. I would bring home about $175 to $200 dollars per outing. Which I felt was pretty good because I was only out 4 to 5 hours per day. Maybe a little longer on weekends, I loved this. Just to think about four months earlier I was just a substance abuser looking for a hit. I had a good head of steam now; I was looking forward to having a clean and sober life.

I was rolling daily, stacking money and feeling good. I had a conscious contact with God and life was good.

I rolled through East Palo Alto one day on that money grind and I saw her.

Wow! I stopped and flagged her down. She was happy to see me. I guess she felt her man, or her trick, her meal ticket, or whatever she felt; but she knew seeing me was a positive thing. I told her that I didn't get high anymore.

That didn't stay that way for long. She was hot; at that point the best I had ever had. I now needed to extend my days or nights anyway. I left the shelter. I quit the school. Now I could sell ice cream all day and get with Denise in the night time. Yes I submitted back to the life again. I guess it was bound to happen. It went well for about two months straight. I would get a hotel room daily. I would get up in the morning, go get my truck and go through the motions; that entrepreneurial stuff. I would stock my product, gas my vehicle and be out on my route. I did my thing; made my money. At the end of the day I had a dealer I would call; tell him what I wanted, and what time I'll be there. I wanted to do this quick because I did not want to leave my truck unattended for very long. I mastered the process of getting my stuff in five minutes or less. Then I would take off. I would get back to the hotel after shutting down my truck. Then I went back to the hotel; to Denise. Of course I came in with everything; the get high, food, money, and a big smile on my face. Yeah I knew I was living a daily life that was only sustainable for so long. I kept this routine.

Then one day I had a problem. Just like other ice cream truck drivers, I had problems with kids jumping onto the back of the truck. One was always concerned with safety. I usually caught kids; and tried to turn them away when I caught them. This one day a young boy jumped onto the back of my truck; and I didn't catch him. I left this particular complex and headed down the street. I passed an ambulance going the other way. I kept going until a police officer stopped me. It turned out that the little boy had jumped onto the back of my truck and I didn't feel him or catch him. He fell off. The ambulance was for him. I was deeply concerned when the cop told me. I stopped early that day and took my truck back to the yard. I just didn't have the heart to go back to San Mateo County anymore. I knew the ice cream company didn't have insurance for me to sell in San Mateo County. I felt like I had made a major problem for them. I never sold ice cream again through that company.

Wow! Now I had an obligation and a habit. Here I go again. I moved back to East Palo Alto.

Things had not changed very much at all; back in 1987 through 1989. During one of those years little East Palo Alto was classified as the most dangerous little city in America. I witnessed a lot of bloodshed. I mean I wasn't an eyewitness but 11 of the people that lost their life there, that one year, were committed on the same street I lived on. The street was called East Okeefe. What it was was a long block full of apartment buildings. I saw ambulances constantly. I kept hearing about people getting shot. I was back using again. Don't want to give a lot more detail because like I said before my next book will detail much of that. Let's just say I did crack things there again daily. Denise came and went. There were other women.

Women were never hard to find because I had a cool spot for people to congregate. Teresa was already in a care facility; so J.R. and I had the house to ourselves.

I lived this life until about 1994. I was now living in San Mateo. I never really used there; but it didn't matter to a substance abuser. It was now near the end of 1993. I had really strong hustle, at this time. I could talk people out of their money with ease. It depended on the type of person. I couldn't scam other substance abuser though.

As a matter of fact I had to keep my wits about me; stay away from the games that were betrayed on the streets. I never got a street name; which would have given me great cover. Everybody had a street name it seemed except me. I knew believe it or not, that if I ever got clean for good I would seek to become a millionaire. I never adopted a street name because I was a loner anyway; few people knew me. I felt that would keep me and tie me to the streets. I wasn't doing much hustle on the street anyway; for anyone to say my name, or street name, to attach it to anything.

I moved from East Palo Alto to a friend of mines; back to the hometown of San Mateo. He lived with his elder Tracy and older sibling. His name was G-man.

G-man was a big guy. He was a cool guy. He seemed to have mastered the cool game. He was also a very confident person. G-man used to have various people come over to his house to use. Tracy worked graveyard shift. In the night time she was not home. In the daytime she stayed pretty much in her room. We would smoke in G-man's room, and also in a couple connecting rooms. It was a pretty cool atmosphere.

I left one day to go to East Palo Alto. I got stuck there for three days using and hustling. I was at another bottom. I took the opportunity to go to detox; awaiting acceptance into my fifth program.

This particular program was hard to get into. There was a waiting list. If one was in a detox already; it showed that one was serious, so one was able to get in quicker. The program I sought to get into was called P90; in San Mateo.

I arrived in detox. The first couple of days I was not asked to do anything, except everyone was expected to keep the room clean. There were plenty of drinks, like coffee, juice, water or milk. Three meals were served per day. The focus was on getting back in one's body the nutrients that were neglected while in our using.

After a few days of just sleeping and eating, I was now regaining my strength.

I did a lot of reading. There were three books that were instrumental to me.

One book was the holy Bible. The next book was a N.A., book. The third book was a book that someone in their infinite wisdom left there. That book was called "Think and Grow Rich".

The think and grow rich book taught me that my future riches are all in my mind. It told me to come up with a definite sum of money that I wanted to acquire.

The sum I came up with was $10,000. The reason I chose $10,000 was because I had received $4000 at once before. I received $5000 at once before; but never had I received $10,000 at one time before.

I stayed in detox for about nine days before being accepted to P90. I came up with the $10,000 figure. I stashed it in my mind; and moved on to P90 to deal with my issues.

P90 was unlike any other program I have been in. I went through the intake. I had my picture taken. I was housed in a clean and sober environment. It was quiet and well kept. No TV watching was allowed during the week. It was just time for self-reflection. I thought about the road I traveled to get there, Wow, another program, number five. What was I going to learn different? What was wrong with me? Was I ever going to end this nightmare? I never continued going to meetings after any of the previous programs. That was a problem in itself.

I slept overnight quietly and peacefully. I was still apprehensive about the program before me. When I was allowed to join the other people in the actual program next door, I arrived at breakfast time. I walked in to see a long line to get breakfast. I was ushered to the front of the line because I was a newcomer.

The concept behind newcomers to a program or N.A. meetings, or A.A. meetings is that newcomers are people with few or no day's sobriety. They are the most important people in attendance. The reason is because as people get clean and sober, there is a tendency to forget some of the pitfalls, the struggles, the down and dirty part of a person's situation.. The newcomers serve to remind people, no matter how much sobriety and clean days they have, where they once were. This may be how one looked when he was a newcomer. That's why people should not get too high and mighty; no matter how much clean time they had. Because one hit, fix or drink takes one back to newcomer status. It serves to be a humbling experience.

One cannot get too high and mighty. It was often said that one may have another fix, pill, hit our drink in them; but another sobriety is not promised.

I got my plate and was pleasantly surprised. The plate was full and appetizing. But as I was eating I recognized him. It was Jerry, nine years older than me. He was my Bernice's age; maybe a little older. He was the older sibling of the man that had my back years earlier when I had the situation with Manny. He was a badder cat then his younger sibling. At earlier times, perhaps 18 to 25 years earlier he was the baddest dude in San Mateo. I wasn't thinking about who he was back then. I was thinking about when I ripped him off for $150 in our past; while using one day.

Fear ripped through my 140 pound body. I didn't know what to expect. He was now looking at me. I remember the day . . . . I was staying in East Palo Alto; perhaps one year earlier. I spent his money and smoked it up. I saw him. I convinced him to give me some credit. I had an uncashed money order for $150. I did that often to stop myself. Because when I had cash I kept smoking until all the money was gone. The money order meant that I would have to stop and think before I got more money. I had to stop and go cash that money order. We were both in San Mateo at a G-man's house. He gave me the dope and I smoked it, and gave others some. He gave me a ride back to East Palo Alto; where we both lived at the time. What I needed to do now was cash that money order and give that man his money. He gave me a ride to the store where I purchased the money order. He waited in the car. That was a mistake on his part. I cashed the money order; and slid my 140 pound frame out the door and hit the long University Ave Street. I made it all the way back to Teresa's house. I slipped away and smoked up the money. I came back later, broke as usual, and began cooking. There was a knock at the door. It was Jerry! He had found Teresa's house because, the guy years ago who gave me my first get high told him where I was staying. He knocked on the door with piercing eyes. He spoke to Teresa, who was sitting in the living room. The respect he had for her overshadowed the anger and disdain he had for me. I got a pass that day from the baddest cat in my city. Now he was here before me.

He didn't say anything to me that day. Two days later he approached me, and told me he wasn't angry at me anymore.. He had been programed for about 45 days at that point. That was part of his sobriety, to let that old debt go. Wow! I escaped another problem.

P90 had much structure, very compact; lots of reading and writing. I was really getting deep into myself I was breezing through the program. Programs were pretty easy for me. I got through the day to day pretty good. I did not make waves; no problems.

Three weeks after I had arrived, word came to me that Bernice had passed. The residents in the program, thugs, misfits and all manner of lowlifes took up a collection with their meager money, for me. The funeral was in Stockton California; where Bernice lived. I now had money to get a round-trip ticket; but I could not leave the program. A former friend of Bernice, who had graduated P90 already offered to escort me to Stockton, to the funeral. I attended the funeral still not knowing what happened to her; why did she die?

Everyone who is a substance abuser has to have a bottom to quit using. A bottom is different for everyone. Sometimes it takes someone one knows who dies.

Sometimes it takes losing a marriage partner; sometimes involving kids. It is different for everyone. I thought my bottom would be Bernice dying. I graduated P90 and moved to a house in the city, called Parker Castle. I was setting myself up for failure again. I wasn't going to any meetings and I had set up shop in a house that housed users. I soon found that out.

I got a job at an recycling center. I was trained to run the whole thing. I was given a choice to operate in East Palo Alto or Redwood City. My mind chose East Palo Alto.

I began by running the recycling site with expertise. I did everything correct.

The process was that people would bring their recyclables; which I weighed the recyclables on a scale and poured them into the appropriate bins. I would then give the people a receipt that would be printed up on a little minicomputer. That computer would add everything; showing how much cans, bottles or plastic they brought; and how much the total was. The receipt gave the customer a grand breakdown and total. It also would give my boss, weights and totals, so that he could know how much were in the bins; and how much money was given out. I would give the receipt to the customer. They would take it inside the store to get their money. I did this job expertly and precisely. I liked this job. I was the man. Until the substance abuser in me saw a way to use. I was about to lose my sobriety again; because I had a new hustle.

I started to use again; and I had a new cash cow; recycling. I begin to tell people in the neighborhood to bring some recycling in, in a bag or box. I would weigh it up and inflate the numbers. I knew they would catch up to me later; but I did not care at that time. I told the people to take the receipt, cash it and bring me back half the money. They might only have brought one or two dollars' worth of recycling, but I gave them a receipt for twenty or twenty-five dollars. They got paid, and I got half.

I racked up. It got so good to me that I begin to print the receipts up at will. The dope dealers began accepting the receipts as cash value. I gave them the receipts as money in the evening after work. The dealer gave me dope, and got their money from the store. I was getting high for free daily.

The manager came by and assumed I was doing such a great job, that he let me open up a site in Redwood City. I went there for couple of days, and found that there were very few customers coming in. I removed a huge book of receipts; and was now mass-producing, filled out receipts with the company seals. I would print about 30 to 40 receipts per day. All had totals of over $24 each.

I did this for maybe 3 to 5 weeks until the manager came by and told me that the bins were too packed, and needed to be emptied. I knew that the gig would be up pretty soon. Three days later the manager told me that the numbers didn't match up. He told me that he had my check. He said I could get my check, be fired, with charges being filed. That was one choice he gave me. He also told me I could let him keep my check, and be fired with no charges being filed. I don't know what happened. Maybe he had to pay out his pocket, but I kept my check and never heard anything anymore from them.

Although I don't feel good about it now, at the time of this writing, but that was 1994; this is 2016.

I was a monster again. I ran and used, and hustled. Things were pretty bleak for the next year and a half.

I was trouble man again. When I was clean, I had the tools, that education, the wherewithal to get a job, and maintain a job. But when I was dirty, I was one of America's worst nightmares; in a financial sense.

My ability to hustle was largely a product of my education. The same education that had me feeling inferior in the black community. The same education that had me filling like a foreigner around my kin in Los Angeles. I could talk most decent people out of their money, and was very good at it. I didn't talk like a dope fiend. I didn't let myself look like a dope fiend when I was hustling. I wasn't breaking any serious laws. I was almost untouchable in terms of backlash. I wasn't going to stick up a liquor store; knock somebody in the head; or even take something out of a store. I would tell fascinating stories to you, pull on your heartstrings, and get your money.

Chapter 5

J.R. Jake and Matt

NOW BACK IN MY home town. I was happy just to have a place to lay my head down. There may have been maybe 2 or three times that I slept in a dried creek area in Palo Alto; with other homeless and dope fiends. For the most part though, I always had a roof over my head. I set out to get my hustle on each day. San Mateo, at this time was much different though. Times and economics were a little bit tighter there. People were not really going for my hustle as much. It was not as easy as I had been used to. I had to venture out further and further. I began walking through to different cities. I would walk from San Mateo to Burlingame; and sometimes into San Bruno; which had to be at least 8 to 10 miles away. This is the reason why I stayed so small; because I had to walk so far away, to make sure that I did not knock on any of the same doors I had maybe knocked on the previous day. These walks became long and tiresome. Then when I did get the money I wanted, I did not have an automatic connection available in San Mateo. I sometimes had to catch the bus all the way back to East Palo Alto. Sometimes after getting my dope in East Palo Alto, I smoked the dope up before getting back to the bus stop. I had to then endure a hour and a half bus ride back to San Mateo. Then I still had a half of an hour walk back to the house. This was now a very hard life I was living.

    I first met Matt after a couple of weeks of living at J.R.'s house. Matt was a white dude that had a fine Mexican girl. Matt had a black Camaro. Matt and I started hanging out together; getting high together and then hustling together. We used to go to San Francisco. There were also about three times that we went to the city, as it is called, with faulty brakes. We would be flying off the hills with little ability to stop. He would use the parking brake to stop. Like I said, I am so lucky to be alive today . . . . Matt moved away about 6 months later. One day I walked to the store on the other side of town: near where I grew up.

I ran into a guy I may have used with once or twice. His name was Dan also. Dan was someone I associated with back in the East Palo Alto days. I did not really know him too well. I did not trust him that well either. Dan asked me if I was looking for some stuff. I had a little money so I told him yes. At that time getting dope in San Mateo was a little harder for me; because I did not have a connection there. Since I did not have a go to person; I decided to get it through Dan's people.

At the time Dan was walking with this big 400 pound man with a street name of "Big man". Dan, Big Man and I began walking back to J.R's place to wait for the connection; his name was Jake. We arrived and set down. We did not have a TV or a TV service so we just filled the time with short conversation. Big Man would take periodic hits with a short pipe he had in his pocket. I started contemplating how I was going to get some more dope out of Big Man.

I slowly began to wear him down. I told him first that I had money I was going to pick up in San Francisco later. I asked him if he could front me some dope. I of course told him that I would pay him back. At first he was not willing.

It seemed that he was leery of the backlash from Jake. I just kept talking and talking. Even though he was trying to make sales, I knew he wanted to smoke more of what he was limiting himself to. I then told him that I would smoke some with him.

That did the trick. Big Man and I smoked up about fifty dollars' worth of dope.

When the dope was gone; I left Big Man there with J.R.; and went to try to hustle up some money. I told Big Man that I was going to San Francisco. I came back later with about twenty dollars. I did not tell him I had any money because I knew I already owed him the fifty dollars. In order to gain some more time,

I told him I had a check coming in the mail tomorrow; in order to buy some time. Tomorrow came and there was no check. Big Man became very scared. He was scared of the reaction he might get from Jake; because there was no dope and no money to show for it. The time came when Jake arrived. Jake knocked on the door. I had come up with a game plan and I hoped it would work. Jake asked Big Man about his money, or his dope. Big Man motioned to me. What I said was not addressed to Jake. It was addressed to Big Man. I said "Big Man we should tell him the truth". Big Man swelled with fear when I told Jake that Big Man and I had smoked up his dope. Jake became just as angry as Big Man was afraid. Big Man said to me "you don't know what you've done man! You don't know what you've done". Jake looked at Big Man with anger and disdain.

He took out his member and relieved himself into a glass. He then poured the rest of the beer into the glass with the urine; before telling us that that glass was for Big Man. Big Man took the drink, and before the night was over Big Man had slipped out the door. I never saw Big Man again. Now Jake needed a new driver. I was now his driver.

I drove him anywhere he wanted to go. I drove him to San Jose, Hayward and all over the Bay Area. One thing I did notice was that Jake always got his money. I remember taking him to a guy's job. Jake showed me his guns. He had a 45 and a 38. He used them to establish fear in the eyes of men. After a few weeks of driving, I grew tired of driving and not getting paid more. I used to talk about the book I was writing at the time. I knew one day I would get clean; despite five failed attempts at programs; and numerous attempts at getting sober on my own.

I went out for a walk. I came back with a game plan. I smoked a lot of dope. I didn't know what the cut was. But I became very paranoid. I got on that 6am bus with people on their way to work. I was sweating a great deal. I got on and found a seat near the rear of the bus; away from the other passengers. I must have looked like Casper the black ghost. My eyes were beaming. I made it to Palo Alto; and made it to the creek. I stayed down there until all the dope crumbs were gone from the corners of my pocket. I stayed down there until I was not high anymore. I decided that day that I had to get out this life and get back in a drug program.

Chapter 6

My 6th program

1996 HAD ARRIVED. I had been in and out of this nightmare since 1984. I was 35 years old now; and approaching another program, P90 again.

This time around I had changed. I was older now. My life was being wasted; five programs and still not clean. My intake to P90 went the same. I stayed at the clean and sober house. I received my intake, and was admitted to the group with the other residents. There was a group meeting that I was a part of; but something happened that I was not expecting.

My group of about 12 people set in a circle. Somebody was getting focused on.

Then they got to me. They told me, they said man you've been in five programs.

What more can we teach you? Why are you wasting our time? As a matter of fact, drop something. Tell us something you never thought you would tell someone else.

Tell us something you swore you would take to the grave. I thought "what the hell do they want me to say?" I thought and thought; and what came out was that, Teresa had been a heavy drinker. She would drink, call the ambulance, yelling, obviously intoxicated. That was very embarrassing to me as a kid. I hid that inside of me. I stuffed that inside of me. I never spoke about it to anyone before that day; before that meeting.

Things flowed pretty easily as the days passed at P90. I definitely began to be more studious.

The format was the same. I breezed through the days and weeks. I made it through the first 30 days. That was the time someone in recovery really needed to be watched and separated from anything that might be a trigger for that person to leave the program for that person to go back out and use.

As a person gets more clean time and more stability, one sees more freedom. I breezed through the program until I got to my 53rd day clean. I was walking to a Narcotics Anonymous meeting; down Ellsworth Street in the hometown. I was walking, and that's when I saw him. He saw me also. He turned left onto the street I was walking on.

It was Jake. He had found me. I knew I had ripped him off a year earlier. I braced myself for my interaction with him. He got out of the car. He stepped to me and confronted me. He said "I want my money man!" "I want my money!" I said man, I'm in a program now.. I'll pay your money when I get out. The anger on his face was intense.

What he didn't know was that I always had very quick hands. Going back to my basketball days, I was completely ready for him to throw a blow. I was ready to block the blow and launch my own counter move. I did not let my face show my attentions. I showed no fear. I spoke to him calmly, precisely. Things had obviously changed within me. I wasn't the hundred and 40 pound guy anymore. I always gained my weight back in programs. This program was no different. I had to be weighing about 225 at that time. I wasn't going to be no pushover. He saw that he could not produce the fear within me that he was used to seeing from everyone else.

He tried another approach. He told me after a couple of seconds of his reflection on the situation that "I got some real good stuff man. I got some real good stuff." I was not looking for or ready for that statement. I sighed and thought to myself, you got 53 days clean. Hell! I wanted 54! I told him "no man I'm in a program now.

That probably shocked him. He probably had never been turned down by a fiend before. But I was not using anymore. Even though I always knew I was one pill, fix, hit, or drink away from being trapped again. After I said that, he looked at me again, he hesitated. He reached out his hand to shake mine. He looked at me and he told me "I respect that". He walked away, and I felt like I had finally turned my back on that life. Time went forward until I graduated P90 again. The staff at P90 wanted to make me a manager at a facility they had in South San Francisco. I did not want to go to South city; as it was called. I decided to stay at one of their clean and sober houses in Redwood City.

There were three bedrooms in the house. There were two residents each in two of the bedrooms. The manager occupied the third bedroom by himself. The manager was just another clean guy; who had more clean time than everyone else. His rent was lower. He just had to make sure everyone kept the house clean; from trash and substances. He collected the rent and maintained the household.

I got a job at a 7-Eleven in Menlo Park. It was cool. I worked the graveyard shift. It was an alright job for the most part. I did keep looking though.

I got another job offer. I accepted a job driving buses for disabled people.. The training was about six weeks long. I completed the training and began driving. I felt so happy and proud that I was finally living life on life's terms. I was ecstatic. I drove the bus for many months. I was finally clean now. I would visit Teresa who was now in a care facility. It felt so good to have her see me in this light.

I moved to Redwood City for a couple of months. I then found a room at a hotel in San Mateo. It was a typical room with the shower down the hall.

One day I was doing my job, driving the bus on my route. I got a call on the intercom telling me to take the bus back to the yard. I guess it makes sense. One would not want to tell someone their loved one passed away, while they were driving clients around. I received the news as well I guess as anyone would. I got in my car to drive home. All of a sudden I just started roaring like a lion in my car, on the freeway. The roar was loud. I really had to exhale some pain from inside. Teresa was gone.

I attended mom's funeral. She actually had two services. Pops set it up so that people in the Bay Area, who loved her there, could come pay their respects. He also set up a service in Fresno; where she was actually buried.

In our family structure, yes Bernice had passed away; but we had not been exposed to a lot of these situations. I did not take to heart the significance of the headstone. I still haven't gotten one for her. Right now at the time of this writing, I will surely get that done soon.

Getting back to 1996, I moved from the clean and sober house; with about six months clean then.. I did 90 days at P90; and another 90 days at a clean and sober house.

One day I was driving my bus, and I had a pickup to be made in East Palo Alto. I rolled in thinking about my past. Just seven months earlier I was running around in another mindset. Now I felt so proud of myself that I was able to exercise those demons. I was a changed man. I took a route to pick up my client taking me right past the house of my ex-wives parents. I rolled past the house thinking maybe I'll get a glimpse of Regina. Sure enough I saw her walking out of her parents' house. She looked good. I stopped and opened the door. When she saw me she was amazed of how I had changed. I had found myself. We talked a little, briefly; and I moved on to pick up my client.

I moved right across the street from the P90 meeting hall. I continued to attend meetings; which I had not done after any of my previous programs. My sobriety continued to grow. I was a regular at meetings; a P90 graduate. I soaked in all the prestige that that gave me. I will always have great respect for the staff and the organization of P90; a great program in San Mateo.

I was taking out the trash one day, and he walked into my building. It was Jake. He had found me again. That's what he did. I had eight months clean and sober now, and wanted nothing to do with him. He approached me talking about the money I owed him. And just to make sure I complied, he was holding onto a precious book I was writing during my addiction. Yes during this 13 year ordeal I would write and type most nights. At the time of the writing of this book August 2016, I am 20 years free of the madness. I am 20 years sober from it. I am focusing on my life; to one day be that million-dollar guy.

Back to 1997, Jake had my book, so Jake had to be paid. I paid him and got my book back. I had 120 typewritten pages of actual situations; stories, and danger; all real-time writing. Yeah I paid Jake to get my book back. But I was never to meet him again. Just like the other so-called players, hustlers, and dealers back in the days. I played them all. Yes this square, with low self-esteem played them. I ripped off dealers and lived by my wits. I used my square ness and lack of street savvy, to put the street savvy people at ease. I never thought I could get over on them; but I did over and over again at the end. But in the beginning and middle I didn't have a clue. My 140 pound self was running for my life. Survival! That is what it was all about; and I was a survivor. I never used that stuff again! I could have found a way to play him; but I never wanted to see him again in life and I never did to this day.

Chapter 7

Living Life On It's Own Terms

DURING THE LATTER DAYS of P90, before I graduated, the second time actually. I met a young lady. She was in a woman's program, at the same time that I was in the men's. We met and hung out at meetings that both our respective programs took us to.

I met a woman friend. We grew to become good friends.

We talked, and she talked me into getting a place to stay together. We ended up getting a one bedroom house on the bottom floor. On the top floor another family lived. We were real good friends; and we were a couple now.

Cindy told me her story. Her last Old man extorted money from her.. She told me that she finally gave in to him. Click, click, click was the sound. She was also there in the house. But she wasn't smoking that day. No one else was in the house except for him and her. Click, click, click was the sound; as her anger swelled and her rage increased. She began to nail the doors and windows shut in the front room. Click, click, click, bang, bang, bang, click, bang, click, bang, click was the sound. He wasn't paying attention. He was focused on his get high. She was thinking of things to do. She told me she went into the room. He was in a cloud of smoke. She found him in that smoke, with a hammer.

She wailed on him for taking the kids away; for extorting money for her kids, his kids.

She told me she did seven years for her situation. She was released and had to do that program she attended while meeting me.

Now we were an item. I helped her get a job driving the bus. She completed the training and did great. I was so proud of her. I bought her a little car from a tow yard. It ran good for a while. Later it needed a water pump. That young lady went out there, figured it out, and put the water pump on her car herself. Wow that was so cool.

We continued to go forward. My past hustle kicked in; and I went and got an old looking ford economize van. It had a dent on the front right side. But it was a very good ice cream truck. So there it was. I worked on the bus from about 4 AM to about 1 PM. I got off work and started selling ice cream in the afternoon.

We were now living our life in our little one bedroom. We were doing just fine.

We both valued our sobriety. We weren't really going to meetings at this time.

But we both had something to be sober for. I had enough. 13 years was enough for me, from about age 23, 24, to the age of 36, 37, a prime zone of a young man's life. I now had over a year and a half clean and sober. I was finally living life on life's terms. I was happy!

I was happy and she was also. Happiness would increase for her, but not for me.

One day there was a knock at the door. I don't remember how he got there; but her young 14-year-old son showed up at the door.

His name was Tom. Tom seemed like a quiet mild mannered young man. He didn't seem thuggish in his nature. He seemed like a decent young man; and he proved to be. He asked if he could stay. I knew the situation. I knew that she had not been with her off-spring for seven years. Surely I could not turn him away. So I let him stay. I told him he had to go to school; that was a must. Tom was doing alright; no major problems. We continued to work driving the buses. I continued to sell ice cream in the early afternoons and into the evenings.

About 4 to 5 weeks later there was another knock at the door. It was her 16 year-old son. He wanted to stay also. His name was Pete. Pete was a little more outgoing than Tom. Tom was a reserved young man. Pete was a heavyset 16 years old; more outgoing and confident than Tim. Pete was a little less respectful than Tom also.

I was not going to cultivate this. I was thinking of things to do. I told him that I wasn't cool about what he was doing; and what he wasn't doing. He told me that I meant nothing to him. I mean nothing to him; and he's eating my food! Oh hell no! I cussed him out the door; and halfway down the street, young ungrateful kid. I mean nothing to you! Okay cool, I was rethinking my situation at that time.

Before I can reroute what I was going to do. The next thing I knew Cindy had driven to San Francisco; and came back with her 13-year-old daughter. She was 5 to 6 months pregnant. Now how the hell could I turn her daughter away? Wow! Now I had a woman and three kids with one on the way; in a one-bedroom. It just wasn't cool for me. I was sympathetic with her reuniting with her kids; but my sobriety was going to be threatened in this situation.

Cindy and I were never going to be married. I liked her a lot because she was a good friend. Yes she was my lover. I wasn't cheating on her. I didn't have a woman across town. I wasn't happy anymore. With only a year and a half sobriety, I wasn't going to leave myself in a situation to where I might use again; because of the pressure of raising a family. Besides she had seven kids. Who knows who was going to show up next? I knew she had a son in foster care that she was trying to get back. I totally understand her wanting to make up for lost time with her kids. I understand her kids wanting to reconnect with their Cindy. Yet I was the odd man out; because it wasn't in my best interest to continue with this set up. Yeah, I was thinking of things to do.

Time move forward and it was time for the young girl to bring the new addition home. I was able to see a video of the birth; for the first time in my life. Wow what a beautiful situation, when she came home, now in this tiny one-bedroom we had six people; including a little one. Time continued to move forward, while I was looking for a proper, respectful way out.

I continued to go to work. I dropped the ice cream sales, because it was taking my whole day away. I got home from work, on the bus a little after 2 PM. By the time I got my truck stocked, and ready to go, it was about 3:30 PM or so.

Pretty good timing for the kids getting out of school, I was making between 75 and $100 a day for the four hours I did each day. But I had no time left in my day. I had to get up at 3:30 AM to make it to work, so I had to cut off my evenings around 8 PM or so. I wasn't happy anymore. So I had to change this life and steer it into the direction I wanted to go. I didn't know how, but I needed a change.

My route included seniors on my schedule; that I would pick up. I would pick up 20 seniors at a time and take them to a senior center. My route also included taking many people daily to the dialysis center. I really loved this job. I loved helping the seniors. I loved taking people to dialysis. They were sick people. I talked to everyone; and built relationships with the regulars. Each day I rolled into the dialysis center around the same time. I saw the same people, the same wheelchair vans, all the same.

One day and then thereafter going forward, I started seeing an old looking van with a couple of black dudes driving. They didn't have transit uniforms; but they were there every day. I watched them, but I didn't know they were watching me also. They offered me a job.

Chapter 8

"A new job"

I CAME INTO WORK one morning about 4am. I picked up my route for that day. It didn't seem much different from any other day. There were always 2 to 3 pickups that were a little different. Different from the 17 to 20 pickups I did each day.

I picked up a young man that was in a wheelchair. He had a helper with him.

This young man had a real tall wheelchair. The seat was very high and stretched to my neck. No problem, I was trained to deal with any type of chair. I took the client, took him up on the lift, and strapped him in. His helper walked into the bus from the front. I drove off to take my client and his helper to their destination. I got there safely, and moved him into position to go down the lift. I noticed he was eating a cookie; and had crumbs wasted on his chest. I didn't think anything of it. I was going down the lift. With his high back wheelchair that stood up to my neck. This restricted some of my vision; but I'm going down the lift with no problem. Quickly, the helper stepped forward while the lift was going down, and spoke to his friend saying "Sam you messed yourself." He then screamed out because it seems he had put his foot underneath the lift. Wow! I took the lift back up so that he could get his foot out. I got my client off the lift, and took him safely to the sidewalk. I went over to the helper and said, "I'm sorry, are you okay?" He kept saying he was fine. I saw him take his shoe off, and his sock off. There were no cuts are blood visible. He put his socks and shoes back on; while assuring me that he was okay. He pushed my client away.

I gathered the paperwork and filled it out. I filled out the incident report forms. That night I turned the incident report in with my time card; like I was trained to do. I went home for the day.

The next day I began working around 4 am. Just about nine or 10am, I received the call that I was to come by the office. They said don't worry about the rest of my schedule; it was being covered. I didn't know what was happening. The last time something like this happened was when Teresa passed away. I went into the office where my boss was waiting for me. It seems that, the helper of the man, I transported on the wheelchair, claimed he was a little more hurt, the next morning.

He calls my bosses, bosses boss. Everything trickled down; and the mess trickled down to me. I was fired! Now almost 2 years clean. I had never been fired from a job. I always did good work. I had quit a lot of jobs; but never been fired. Yeah, but I was fired now.

It seems they said I didn't make out an accident report. They said that was the proper report to make. I made out an incident report. An accident report I thought was to be filled out when I had an accident. I thought that when somebody hit my bus, or I hit somebody with my bus, that was an accident. What my boss was saying was that I should have filled out an accident report. With an accident report the procedure is to call it in on the intercom. People from the company would come out and take pictures; document everything, so that they could cover their backs later; to cover them from liability.

I left the office a little angry and confused. I then remember a week earlier, I have received a job offer from the guys with the ugly van. I was in awe that they had their own company; and I took the job.

They actually paid me a couple hundred dollars per month more than I had been receiving. Of course there was no medical or dental.

The union that the company had was very small. They didn't get a lot of respect. That little union stood up tall and called me. I met with the union representative. He was a very short black man in statue. But he had a big booming voice like he was 6 foot 9. He assured me that they were going to represent me. I was also helping them too because a win with me would increase their stock, their recognition.

They took the case and got the story. I told them what happened. They did the research, got the documents from the company, and went to work. I went to work for the other company. I won't mention the name of that company.

About 2 to 3 months went by. The new company was expanding because the two black dudes were about their business; hooking up new clients, professional and friendly. It was just like their slogan;

safe, friendly and reliable. I was a very good employee. The dialysis center which made up most of their clients kept feeding them more and more clients. One day they called me in and said they were going to bump my salary up from 1400 per month to 4000 per month. I was happy as heck! I had a big Kool-Aid smile on my face. They then told me the rest. I was now responsible from 4 am to 11 pm; 6 days per week. I had one, two, and three hour breaks throughout the day; but I was responsible. The owners lived in Sacramento, which was about 45 minutes to one hour away; northeast of where we were. I had responsibility for the whole thing. I was responsible for the whole company. I was now making them a ton of money.

They moved forward, expanding their business. They purchased two way phones; that also included a walkie talkie. Perfect! I could communicate with them immediately.. I was the driver. I was the only driver. I was the general manager. I ran the whole show. I started with about eleven clients to pick up for $4000 per month. I loved my job. I loved serving the people. Yeah, loved the job, loved the responsibility, and loved the pay.

Chapter 9

"Meeting the Warrior Queen"

I WAS RESPONSIBLE FOR that company six days per week. I was getting a little bit burnt out because I didn't have much bang in my social life again. Hell I didn't even have much time for a social life. The time I did have was not very exciting. I was making a lot of money now. At that time making $4000 a month was a lot of money for me, a former substance abuser now living a decent life.

I started to reach out to Mitch in Fresno. His name is Mitch. Mitch was Nate's son. He was not Teresa's son. Mitch was the young man that came up to the bay area almost 30 years earlier to see Nate. I reached out to Mitch because I was seeking blood relatives. I was seeking to get to know Mitch. Arnold was living in the Central Valley, somewhere in Modesto. Modesto is only about an hour and a half southeast of the bay area.

As a matter of fact I had not spoken to J.R. since he told Jake where I stayed. I didn't hold that against him so much. It was just that I had to protect my sobriety. I couldn't allow myself to be around any loaded people.

One day I decided to roll down to Fresno. Mitch was giving a birthday party for his mate Laverne. I didn't want to take Cindy with me. Hell I thought I might meet someone there. I knew I was never going to marry Cindy. This was not a romance written in the stars. She was a good friend, my lover, but she did not have the outside beauty I was seeking. I did respect her, and treat her well. There were just too many, complications going on; with the growing responsibility. I was not ready to raise that big a family, that soon, in my sobriety. After all, it was said in the NA, AA, rooms that if one wants to protect his sobriety; one should not get into a relationship within the first two years. I had already disregarded that suggestion. I needed to be happy. I wasn't totally happy in that relationship. Yeah she was not a looker. That matter as much then, just having someone who cared about me. That was important; but I knew that we not going to get married. I probably would have cheated with the first beautiful woman that showed me attention.

I remember when I first introduced her to a friend of mine. On his face I saw his disapproval. Which didn't matter a whole lot; but there was always open competition between us peers.

So Cindy filled a need at that time in my life; and I filled a need in hers. I gave her security, friendship, intimacy, and I was a damn good provider.

She knew what was up. She was putting her life together also.

So I got into the car, and started off on this two and a half hour journey to the southeast of Cali; to the Central Valley. I arrived around 7 PM or so. Mitch lived on the west side of Fresno. Fresno was not a well-liked town to me.

Although I had not gave it a chance. I saw it as to countrified. I was from the suburbs, and that was what I was used to. The west side was one of the poor areas of Fresno.

I pulled up, parked and went inside. I wished Laverne a happy birthday. I gave her a big hug and a hearty happy birthday. She smiled and told me thank you.

I walked into the backyard where they had set up tables, chairs, and nightlights.

They really had it looking good back there.

I really didn't have the relationship I wanted with Mitch; but I was willing to cultivate one.

I sat down at a table; and of course at that time I wasn't drinking.

Although drinks were all around me, I had learned the previous two years to live life on a natural high. I knew the triggers and I didn't want any parts of going back to my former life.

I sat at a table where a young man perhaps 15 years my junior was sitting. We struck up a conversation. I found him to be a fascinating young man. He seemed to have the purest heart I had ever seen in anyone. I was impressed with this young man's demeanor. We talked for 30 or 40 minutes; good, honest, refreshing conversation. There was none of the shallow conversation one gets from a lot of people; especially some younger folks.

Now this next part I want the readers to know, even though it may sound like a cartoon; it may sound like a fantasy; but . . . . She walked into the backyard. The whole backyard, and everyone in it, seemed to turn gray.

Everyone seemed to lose their color; no matter what they were wearing. She was the only person that was in color at that moment. I I thought, this must be what love at first sight feels like. I was pleasantly surprised. She seemed to float across the room. Her smile brightened the dark, grey background. Time itself seemed to freeze. I saw nothing else but her. The dogs barking next door faded out. The lights seemed to get brighter. No! It was a glow that was coming from her!

I had written this poem, a few years earlier in my life. One day I was lonely and asked myself what kind of woman did I want? So I wrote a poem.

"5 Qualifications"

I was asked many times

What do I want in a woman what would suit me fine

I was so lonely any woman would do

The qualities I sought

I never knew but experience brought wisdom and many women so fine

I have five qualifications whoever meets them blows my mind one is the ultimate far above the rest she must seek God and let him be her quest two is serious and very severe she must be clean and sober to keep her focus clear

Three is kind of special

And depends upon me

Beauty's in the eyes of the beholder and beauty's number three

But beauty is strange there's beauty outside and within

It's also something you can see in a friend for intelligence is a must it all starts in the mind what blessings galore if she's intelligent and fine

Five dedicated to the struggle last but not least if I'm pursuing someone who's not dedicated

I might as well cease

I watched her as she began to mingle with her friends and kinfolk.

I looked at the young man I was talking to. I asked him who she was. He looked me right in the eyes; and told me who she was. He said it proudly.

He knew I was excited to see such a beauty.

They young man and I, talked a little bit more; as I continued to keep my eyes on this beautiful queen!

She moved from the backyard into the kitchen area. I asked Mitch to tell me something about her. He began to talk to me about what he knew, about her financial situation. Finances were not my chief concern at this point. Laverne then introduced her to me. I was all smiles. She had a perfect looking smile on her face. Much about her was perfect! She had an excellent figure; with little fat. But she was P.H.A.T. In a sense, because she had that pretty hot and tempting fatness about her. I introduced myself, tried to be as cool as I could be.

I don't remember much of the conversation. But I do remember exchanging numbers. I also gave her a ride somewhere. I do remember she had been in an auto accident recently. Her driver Jackson which turned out to be her sibling's mate had gotten into an accident. He got out and ran. She was in that car. That was kind of going on at that time in her life. I found out years later what had transpired.

I was jazzed beyond belief, as I made my way back to the bay area. I was on a pretty good natural high as I pulled up into my driveway.

At that time cell phones were extremely expensive; especially long distance calls. I would get off work and grab a roll of quarters. There was a pay phone near my home. I got off work every day, six days a week; stop at that laundromat, kick my feet up on a chair; and call this amazing woman.

We had started a long distance romance over the phone. I knew she enjoyed these conversations just as much as I did. We stayed on the phone usually 2 to 2 1/2 hours.

Days went by and I was living on cloud nine. I was floating around work and home but no one knew why.

I made the trip again. We went to the movies and out to dinner. We had a great time. We just clicked. I think she was becoming smitten by me, because of my education and intelligence. Yes, the same education that had me feeling like a foreigner in Los Angeles some 18 years earlier was the same education that was a negative to me on the streets.

I don't want to say that Fresno didn't offer men with education; but in her circles she had not met a man like me. Even though she was one of those women that could get any man she wanted. She was that, outstanding!

I was told years later that her former mates were all thugs.

I was not a thug. I did not want to fake anything. I was what I was.

We were talking every day on the phone. We got to know each other well enough to continue to want to see each other.

At home, I was maintaining, keeping things going, maintaining my part, of the household unit. Yet one thing had changed. I was no player at that time in my life. My feelings had shifted. I had found a queen now. My thoughts and feelings were about her. I never had relations with Cindy again. It might sound a little crazy; but the queen was going to be mine. I was determined. Relations with Cindy was not even in my mindset anymore. I laid in my bed next to this woman; while my thoughts only stayed on this queen who happened to stay in Fresno.

Things had not changed much at home. It did get better for me though. The guys who I worked for got an office set up in Redwood City. It had two bedrooms and a kitchenette. I asked them if I could stay at the office.

That question was asked of them shortly after I found out that Cindy's daughter had qualified for Social Security. Yes sir! That meant that more money was coming into the house. It was not my money. But that money concerned Cindy, and her daughter. That made it easier for me to leave. That meant Cindy could maintain without me financially. I did shed a tear because I had deep like for Cindy; and I did have staying power; from years earlier; Nate showed me how. This was not the time or place though.

I had to go.

It was now time for Cindy to reconnect with her kids. Cindy knew it too. She didn't want me to go; but she knew it was the time in her life to reconnect with her kids. We said our goodbyes; and I moved into the office. I didn't feel like I abandoned her. I feel like I left her in good standing; because she would be financially able to take care of her kids.

The owners agreed to let me stay in the office rent free. That was a part of my deal. I was starting a good foundation for my life now. I was financially stable; making over 4000 a month with no rent in the bay area. I only had two years sobriety, but as they say in the clean and sober community, a day at a time. I knew in my heart that I would never smoke that mess again. I want the readers to know that at the time of this writing August 2016 I am 20 years free of what I used to do. The time was 1998 when I moved into the office. For those who may be suffering with substance abuse; I want to let you know that it can be done. I did it and continue to do it one day at a time. I was so happy at this time in my life. I was making good money. I was in control of the whole damn thing. I was rolling with this good feeling, when some more good news came at me. Cindy came to see me; and told me that the union rep was looking for me. It seemed I had won my case against the old company.

I went to see the union representative. He informed me that I had won over $17,000. I was obviously presently surprised! I was mapping out a strategy in my mind about what I was going to do.

When I went to pick up the check from the old company; I saw my former boss. He stood there with that look on his face. He had a lot to say to me; and he had a lot to say to the arbitrator that decided the case. But there he was looking at me speechless. His jaw was dragging on the ground. Surely someone's head had to roll on this one. They set it up for my head to roll. But it looked like it would be his head rolling like a big wheel.

When I went to get the check though, it was only for $10,000 and some change. It seemed taxes were taken out first; and they took seven grand! I did know that I would be getting that seven grand back in my next year's income tax return. So I thought at that time.

I did not realize it then, but that $10,000 figure was the same figure I had in my mind in that detox two years earlier! Let the readers think about that clearly! I learned that this was not a coincidence! I wish I had known that then. I had forgotten about that 10,000 figure. But it was still in my subconscious! Readers are going to have to do their own research. But our riches are in our mind! The only thing I can suggest once again is that everyone get a copy of the book "Think and Grow Rich". Priceless!

Now August, September, 1998, I was in full power. The readers have gotten the idea of what it took for a young man with low self—esteem, former high school scrub, college scholar, substance abuser, lonely, depressed, and was ready to step to a queen; to be able to offer her a life to rein together as one.

I continued to call Tina, the queen on a daily basis. By the way, I did give Cindy $1000 to help her out. She was a good woman. But Tina was in my sights. I wanted and needed that queen in my life. I wanted the best. I had thrown away so much of my life; up to that point. I wanted the best of everything. I had deprived myself for years. I often settled for second best.

Not anymore. I knew and felt ready; and I was coming to get my queen!

At first I had not mentally and financially set the foundation for my throne; and the queen's throne.

I put the majority of my money in the bank of course. I looked at my credit report and saw that all the years of using, and the time involved had allowed my credit to clear. I already had a couple of grands. So here I stood with 12,000 in my savings, with 4000 a month coming in as income. I had that credit. I got 3 secured credit cards for a thousand dollars each.

The new potential queen and I developed a whirlwind romance. It was quick and it was passionate! I would go down to Fresno as often as I could.

We did the normal things like movies, clubs, casinos, and dinners. We ate at red lobster often. That was our favorite restaurant. I put a down payment on a new car. I traded in the ice cream truck. I kept my little ford pickup that I only payed $400 for; at a towing yard.

I came down to Fresno often. Now it was time for her to come visit me. I wanted to inspire confidence in her that I was the real thing. I brought her, her five-year-old that she was raising since birth and the young man that I met at my Laverne's party the one that told me who she was. Wow! As it turns out He was her off-spring.

All four of us drove back to Redwood City; to stay a couple of days. Oh! It was great! I showed her parts of the bay. The bay area didn't need much of a sales job from me. The bay will always be the bay; my hometown forever. I love the bay area. We went back and forth over the next couple of months.

We had great conversations. I got to check out her spiritual level, her educational level, and her business mindset. She was not ghettofied; which I didn't want or need in my life. I didn't want or need any drama in my life.

It was about November 1998 when I brought her up to the bay area; and we got a hotel room. Yeah we could have stayed at the office. But I wanted to provide her with a little more flair. We got a hotel room in Redwood City. It was about $100 a night, or maybe a little more.

This hotel had a Jacuzzi in it. We made passionate love that night! I posed the question," will you marry me". The answer came back yes, to a background of the song Midnight Woman. The happiness, the freshness, the joy, the harmony, I was truly happy to the fullest for the first time in my life.

I felt like I had all the foundation I needed. I didn't want, seek, or need street life anymore. I paid my dues. The low self-esteem was pushed down deep. It was not to come back for over a decade. Financially I was good. My throne waited. We set a marriage date for December 3, 1998.

I remember the air being fresh every day. It was like that going back to school feeling. One had their new school clothes. You were ready to get it started.

I was ready to get it going. She was one of the finest women I had ever come across; or at least had the confidence to step two.

I told her she didn't have to work. I told her I would carry the financial day.

As we were driving back to Fresno, my mind was focused on the coming days, weeks, and months. This had to be right. I set my sights on the work I needed to do. I had so much go wrong in my life before her. I just wanted to get it right. I thought about everything, even to the smallest detail.

I know it must have been a shock to her family. Who is this guy from the bay that seemed to knock her off her feet? Who was this guy that came in and swooped her up?

Yeah it was I. Coming to get his queen. She started making her plans. I started making my plans. The big day finally arrived. We got married at City Hall in Fresno California. Mitch and Laverne where the witnesses. It was short and sweet. I was happy and she was happy.

I moved her as planned back to the office in Redwood City. I also moved her son, Harry; the young man I was talking to when I met her. Harry was a very welcome young man. He helped Tina with whatever she needed. He was a truly great son. I think Harry was about 24 at that time.

Harry as I was told had spinal meningitis when he was a very young. One of the effects was that he was very short in stature. But he was also very big in love.

I believe Tina told me that they had to put a stunt up his back.

Although he had that beginning, and that past; he still had one of the purest minds and heart I had ever seen. It was a pleasure to know him and be near him. She also brought with her another young man who was the age of five.

His name is Earl. Earl was a super great kid at the age of five. What I did understand was that Earl was her nephew. She raised him from birth. Tina took him from birth and raised him as her own. A fantastic kid he was, and proved to be.

So there it was. The four of us moved to the great city of Redwood City. I would get up and go out six days a week; putting in work; taking the seniors, and handicapped, to and from dialysis; and other medical appointments. I worked six days a week; so I was hoping things would not get boring for her and them each day. I stayed in work provider mold; just like Nate did. Tina was the homemaker supreme. Boy! Could that women cook! Every evening when I came home, dinner was hot and ready.

One day I ran into my old friend G-man. He and I grew up in San Mateo. I guess I considered him a best friend; but I knew him to be a little bit two faced. G-man met my wife and his jaw dropped. Yet, the total opposite look on his face, from the time he met Cindy. Yeah I loved it! G-man and I had always had somewhat of a competition. Yet be that as it may be, I was winning the battle of the best looking mate. He had just gotten out of the penitentiary. He didn't have a girl at that time. Even if he did, no doubt that she would not be able to hold a candle to my woman. Tina was the girl you did take home to momma. Too bad Teresa was already gone. She would have loved this girl. Yeah G-man walked away jealous that day.

As days moved into weeks, I tried to keep things a little bit exciting. This was somewhat difficult because of the fact that Tina had never learned to drive. No mate she had before me had ever wanted her to drive. I didn't share that same mindset. I guess they wanted to keep her in the house. But I got a new lease on life. And I wanted her to have everything I had, or was going to acquire. I got a new lease on life and I wanted her to have everything I did.

I set out to teach her to drive. I started off teaching her myself. We would go by empty parking lots, to make sure she didn't hit anything. She did all right. She was a little bit apprehensive. But she was getting better. Yeah we shared a lot of laughs about her driving instruction. I soon started taking her to driving school with the professionals. Next thing I knew my lady got her license! I was so proud of her. I bought her a little Maverick for her first car. I would buy her many cars in the future; but this was her first car. She looked real good in it too. I was so happy with my little family. I was working hard so that I could keep things popping for my little family. I thought things were going real well for a couple of months. I had huge plans.

The people, the clients I was driving which stood at about 17 people at that point, didn't recognize the company as much as they knew me. I had real personal relationships with all my clients. 17 clients at about $900 each month was what the company was getting. I was instrumental with helping the company receive over $15,000 per month. They were paying me four thousand dollars per month; plus staying at the office rent free.

One of the owners was a tall black dude. He was cool as hell. He had a real good attitude with a good moral foundation. His name was Isaac.

Anyway Isaac was a good man and we always had a good relationship. He was a partner in his company with another young man whose name was Zack. Zack was what I would call bosie. I don't want to hold that against him; but I did. I didn't like the way he used to look down on me and other black people in general. He had the air of thinking he was better than everybody else. We did not see eye to eye a lot of times. Nevertheless he was my boss; although 10 years my junior. It took everything in me to give him the respect that his position required from me.

As was said earlier, my understanding was that I made $4000 per month, which I broke down to a paycheck every other Tuesday. Math was, and will always be my best subject. He tried many times to treat me like a sucker. He tried to change my pay schedule. I will break it down. I was getting paid every other Tuesday $2000. When you spread that out to all year; you start off with 52 weeks in a year. Since I got paid every other week, that's 26 times I would get paid in a year; amounting to a total of 52,000 per year.

Wow! Two years removed from a 13 years of ignorance; and now I'm making $52,000 per year. Zack moved to change my pay schedule from every other Tuesday to two times per month. The difference is that, I set every other Tuesday means $2000 times 26 pay periods equal $52,000 per year; all day every day. He wanted to change my pay period from every other Tuesday, and the 26 pay periods per year; to twice a month. Twice a month times 12 months means 24 pay periods. He tried to slip that pass me. So he wanted me to miss the fact that he was taking $4000 out of my pocket. This was just one of his tricks he tried to pull on me. I wasn't going to let that happen. Like I said math will always be my best subject; with writing being a close second. He was trying to treat me like a sucker. I built that company with my hard work. That pay cut that he hid wasn't going to get past me. With Isaac's sound advice to Zack; that pay cut wasn't going to happen. Weeks went by before Zack stepped to me; after coming back from Sacramento; saying that he felt since I had my family in the office, he wanted me to pay $500 per month rent. I understood his logic. I was the man now. A man had to have his responsibilities. I understood his logic; but that wasn't our deal! Stayed at the office rent free was the foundation. Why change now, so that you can get other money from me? So he can get that pay cut even bigger now? $500 per month times 12 months equals $6000. I felt like I did nothing wrong in my work to take a pay cut. I was making them over $11,000 a month net. They were constantly adding more work to my schedule. I was still responsible for that company 4 AM until 11 PM; six days per week. If I got hurt or injured I was in a deep mess. I had no medical or dental insurance. If I got sick they had to make their way from Sacramento to cover me. I never got sick. I was impeccable in my work.

Zack kept pushing that $500 per month rent real hard. Now I was thinking of things to do.

My original goal was to set up the foundation of my kingdom, with my new queen right there in the bay. My kingdom, I knew my way around. I set my sights on establishing my own company. I knew a number of clients were coming with me. Everyone has a choice right?

At the same time my queen, my wife did not seem like she was happy as I wanted, or needed her to be. I was all into her and the two young men.

Yeah Harry was not a kid; but he was her son. I loved that young men mainly because of his demeanor, and the fact that he was Tina's firstborn son. I was thinking of things to do. I started to think deeper on my personal business. I got Isaac to bring up some paperwork for me. I solidified my position at the bank. I began to call real estate agents. I figured that Zack wasn't going to stop with this $500 per month situation. Yet my pride was bruised. Maybe I should have thought things over more thorough. I felt disrespected, because I fulfilled everything I was supposed to do in my daily assignments. I was impeccable, never late; with the traffic in the bay area that was a tall order in itself.

The icing on the cake that fueled my departure from that company was the fact that Tina didn't seem to be as happy as I wanted her to be.

She couldn't tell me what was on her mind. My assumption was that she missed not only her other off-spring in Fresno; but her grandkids as well. That was beyond what I could control. I then made the decision to move.

Chapter 10

A new homeowner!

I DECIDED THAT IF I was going to move to Fresno; and pay rent there, I should inquire, or at least set myself up to be a homeowner. This idea took a lot of work that I had no training for; instructions for or knowledge of. Yet I was ready to go. I owned it to myself; and my new queen to get it right. I could not afford to lose my shirt on this one. There was just too much at stake. I inquired with real estate agents. I made sure I was in good standing with my bank. My money was tight. Like Nate told me years earlier when I was rolling along in college. He told me "D. L., I hear that you are making good money, and rolling along in college". I said yeah pops, I'm doing well. I have three part-time jobs, I'm getting school financial aid money. I got a "b" average. I'm doing okay. he did ask me if I was stopping some of that money.

I asked him what he meant. He asked me if I was saving some money. I said no pops. I said I'm taking the girls out, having a good time. He said "son if you're not stopping some of that money, you may as well not be making it."

My pops, with only a sixth grade education, but that knowledge he had was supreme.

I had stopped some of my money 18 years later. I now had about $17,000 in my hip pocket. I had honored his words; set myself up for some longevity.

It took all I had in me to do this on the job training. I was positioning myself to be an homeowner. Something my father always preached. I remember when he lost his home, our home. He finally fell behind in his mortgage payments. At this time J.R. was working and doing big things.

He had a damn good job. He had saved thousands. Pop found out later after losing his house, that he could have gotten the money from J.R. to keep his house. He never asked J.R. I never inquired of pops about his money. He just always seemed to have money. He was a tremendous hustler. He was a mega hustler. I was a teenager then, working, but didn't have any idea about the complexities of home ownership.

I was putting everything in place. The bank foundation was done; my credit was right, that was done; I had secured the money to cover what was ahead of me. I had set the foundation. The bank approved me for a loan of over a hundred thousand dollars to purchase a home in Fresno. Before that though, I passed up a great opportunity. It was a rookie mistake. There was a property available with 3 units on the property. There was a three bedroom house and two two-bedroom units available on the lot. The lady I talked to on the phone told me that the other two houses will pay the mortgage. I should have consulted Nate, who was now in Fresno. I didn't talk to him that turned out to be a big mistake. I know he would've told me to take it. I didn't take it. I passed it up. I did find another house that I was going to take in Fresno. I took Tina down to see it. It had a swimming pool; which she liked. She could see the grandkids swimming and having fun. I just wanted her to be happy. We settled on that house and I went forward. The lady told me that they were going to put a tent on it. She said the house had termites. That put up a red flag for me. Termites! I didn't want to deal with that. I quickly pulled out of the deal. I did find another house though. It was in a good area of North Central Fresno. It was in an all-white neighborhood though.

It was a corner house. It was a beautiful three bedroom home.

I do admit that a lot of these decisions were made quickly but I was blinded by love. If I had taken time to make more intellectual decisions, I would not have moved to Fresno. I would have stayed with my first mindset. I would have stayed; and built up my kingdom in the bay area. I did not do that though; even though everything was set up for success.

The move to Fresno was huge! There were a lot of pieces that had to be put in place.

Mitch got a small loan from me, of about $150 to pay his cable bill. He was having a problem paying me back. I wasn't low on funds but I wanted my money back. Since he had not paid me I came up with an idea. I figured he could pay me back with sweat equity. Therefore I had him come to the office the night before to help me move. Incidentally at the time of this writing January 2016, my brother Mitch submitted to his lower nature with jealousy and anger; because I would not give him a loan for $5000.

Anyway Tina's other son Terry came to help us out, and to drive one of our vehicles.

At this time I had Tina's maverick, my ford that I financed, the wheelchair van I had purchased from Zack; and also the U-Haul.

Tina's 17-year-old daughter, Nancy and her mate also took part in this migration. We all found someplace to sleep in the two-bedroom office; the night before. We woke up the next day, the move day, and I found that Mitch was already up and working. I will always give him mad props for that. We got the truck packed; and were getting ready to set the guidelines for our departure.

We set out driving from Redwood City in a 4 car caravan; to make it to the great city of Fresno California. Almost 30 to 45 minutes into our journey, I looked into my rearview mirror and I saw Terry had passed me up on the shoulder of the road. There were sparks coming from underneath Tina's car. He pulled over and fortunately all four vehicles were able to recognize what was going on. We all stopped to assess the situation.

Obviously that maverick wasn't going to make the journey. I had to get a tow truck to tow the car off the freeway. I towed the car to an U-Haul place. I purchased the trailer to pull the maverick along. Hours were going by. It took time to get the tow truck. It took time to get the trailer and car hook up; and to get back on our journey. I found out later that the wheelchair van was having a hard time making the journey also. The wheelchair van had a hard time keeping up with the freeway minimum speed. I had purchased that van from Zack's crooked self. It turned out that the wheelchair van had some engine issues. I got the van from Zack in return for the $1500 he owed me.

We were using Nextel phones, with the walkie-talkies included. I was happy when those phones were purchased. They were a great help for me to do my job. I could always contact the owners by walkie-talkie. Zack though, even though he was a married man, had so much money coming in; that he was calling a woman in another state, constantly.

This was at a time when portable phones were extremely expensive; especially long distance calls. He ran that Nextel bill up very high. The plan had three users on it; Isaac, Zack, and myself. The total bill was over $2000. $1500 of that bill belonged to Zack. I had put the bill in my name at that point. I don't remember why. Zack was slow about coming out with the $1500 he owed me. So he basically gave me this van. I accepted, because that was my original idea, for me to build my kingdom, my empire in the Bay Area. I was going to take most of his clients that were loyal to me; not to the business.

Anyway I dealt with all these situations on this journey; making the almost 3 hour trip that turned into seven hours. My aim was to keep that level of living high! I set out on all levels to solidify my foundation. I had to keep Tina happy. After all I told her she didn't have to work. She really didn't push that statement; or stand firmly on it. It was me that wanted to keep my word.

The problem was that I told her that on the basis that we were going to be living in the bay. Fresno was a whole different situation. Looking back now, I know I should have consulted her about more things, I know things would've been different. I don't blame her for anything though. I set out to do what I obligated myself to do.

Keeping my financial mindset was extremely important. I soon found that they were a lot of expenses that I had not put much thought or even considered. I needed to buy furniture to fill in the rest of the house. Tina's stuff that we took to the office was not enough to fill that house. I bought new things as needed. I had no income at that time. I had goals, dreams but no income. I wasn't extremely concerned. I did have great money management; and so did she.

Days turned into weeks. It was now 1999. 1999 was a very good year.

Our first year was supreme. I didn't care that I was in a rural city. I didn't care that it wasn't the Bay Area. I was in love and nothing else mattered. I was happy. I had the queen; and everybody else had to shut up. I was happy!

The queen was beautiful! She was great at everything she did. She was a natural beauty. She was a perfect role model to her kids, grandkids, and any kid that was in her general surroundings. She was the honeypot during the whole time we were married.

The queen! Yes she was beautiful. She was a short woman about 5 feet four. My black queen was a brown skinned woman that never needed to wear makeup. She only wore lipstick. A natural beauty she was; fine, weight proportionate to her height. She moved with the grace of a gazelle.

She did have some of her own income. Her son Harry was receiving Social Security because of his condition. She also had money coming in for Earl. Therefore I didn't worry too much about money in her purse. I just make sure that the money she had she could spend as she wanted. She always spent money on the household anyway.

I was going forward and spending money out of my savings, and credit cards in order to keep the house afloat. I was spending a lot of money, trying to get that van and my business going; in order to get my money flow income from the business. I stayed optimistic. Even though the circumstances I had put myself into were not ideal.

Year 1 was going well. Things were intense; but I was very much in love. I wasn't even feeling the pressure yet. I just kept making moves to keep us living a high level. I was becoming hustler supreme. I was turning into a new kind of dude. I was going to keep his family afloat by any means necessary. That means I had to do some things that I had to do.

Wow 1999! New Year's come and went. Things were fresh. I was a proud homeowner. A proud man, I was. I felt so fortunate to have a queen.

I was very jazzed. Money was going out of the household; but we stayed afloat. Tina had money, so she was good. I was operating without using any of the money she had coming in. So she was financially good.

I was looking forward to the $7000 I was getting back from my income taxes; from the settlement check I received much earlier.

The way things went down the settlement was structured to give me money I would have received, had I continued to work for the company that fired me. If I had been on the payroll and was continuing to work for that company I would have received $17,000 for that yearly body of work. What happened was that since the check was added up into one lump sum; taxes were taken out based on that lump sum. Normally I would not have been taxed $7000. That became the total taxes that were taken from me. Anyway I was expecting to get that $7000 back when I filed my taxes. I had always done my own tax preparation. This particular year since I was married, I filed married filing jointly; even though Tina had no taxable income. I filed my taxes and went about my life; waiting for that $7000 to come in. I guess the reader can imagine my shock, when there was no $7000 coming. The IRS took my money for something I did not do. What the hell were they talking about! I had no kids. No support should have been taking from me. I felt like there had to be some mistake.

Nancy, Tina's daughter, at 17, moved into my Cat's sibling's house and started receiving assistance. I guess she must have gotten over $7000 worth of benefits; because since I filed married filing jointly,

IRS in their infinite wisdom took that $7000 from me; and I guess gave it to the back support.

Yeah I was angry. What a screwed up start to 1999. That really set the year up as a financial problem; at the beginning. Nancy made it easy for me to be angry about the situation, because we were not getting along. We continued to be at odds with each other. I guess she wanted Tina to marry some thug based dude. That was not me.

Usually thugs put hands on women. That's what a lot of thugs do. I know, not all of them; but by what I heard years later, was that Nancy was really close to her Old Man a little more background on what I came to understand about Tina's background. My wife was a southern peach!

From my understanding she was married to a man. She had one off-spring already. That was the young man Harry; with this man, she had two more; Nancy and Terry. Terry was Tina's second son.

She then had Nancy. Tina told me he was a very jealous man to his beautiful wife. I do understand that. She was a gorgeous woman. I do understand his jealousy. But to go upside her head and abusing his son was something I wasn't about. From what I heard he was a workaholic; but to put hands on someone he claimed to love; that's crazy. He was a real thug though. I was not. I was kind of a gentle giant. I was not a tall guy. I was a big guy though. I just thought the reason she did not like me was because I was unlike him.

I had to accept the fact that I would not have that seven grand to start this coming year. Yeah, I was mad at Nancy. That was in effect. But I should have been angry at myself. I found out years later that there was a way I could have gotten that money back.

Nevertheless my anger at Nancy subsided; even though we never got along much of the time; when I came in contact with her. I really would have loved to have a better relationship with her. It wasn't to be. So I tried to ignore her as often as I could. We would have many verbal battles in the coming years.

Now here was 1999. I can see that things were going to be tight if I didn't do something outside the box. The credit cards were getting low. The cash savings was being consumed monthly. I managed to keep us afloat.

From the outside looking in, it looked like we were living the American dream.

It's like looking at the pond and one sees a duck on the water.

It seems to be moving so gracefully. It seems like the duck is not even breaking a sweat in a sense. Little movement, at ease, just so little effort, and most people would say wow look at that, that duck is so at peace. Now I want to take the camera and put it right on the water's edge. One would see that that duck is paddling like hell to stay afloat, little feet moving back and forth working hard.

That was me! That duck, everything looking good, looking fine from the outside. New furniture, bills paid, food stacked in the freezer, steaks, lobsters, shrimps, crabs, at our immediate disposal. Tina was looking good.

The kids were living free and unhindered by financial pressures. We were living way beyond our means; but nobody knew it but me. Tina didn't even know the total financial meltdown that was occurring. I didn't want her to know though. I just kept re-creating myself over and over again.

Anyway, the anger about Nancy had to subside. Anger at her, wasn't going to put money in my pocket. I had to make a move.

An opportunity presented itself to me to get a quick 3000 bucks. One of the former owners of the company, I used to work for, came to me with a proposition. It was Zack. I should have told him to kick rocks but I listened.

He proposed that I finance a Range Rover for him on my credit and he would give me $3000. Yeah I know it was a dumb move; but I had a lot of pressure on me to keep things afloat.

I took the deal. It was Terry who I took with me. At this time Terry and I had a good foundation of a relationship. He was young, perhaps in his early 20s. We rode up to the bay area from Fresno.

Terry and Zack didn't seem to like each other at all. Zack had purchased an outfit; I believe by Calvin Klein. It was a warm-up suit. I found out later that Terry had taken it from Zack's car. That theft, that I didn't even do, came back to haunt me sometime later.

We arrived at a credit union in the Bay Area, the same credit union that I had financed my car at, the same credit union that I had good standing with. I went right in there. They wanted about a $3000 down payment.

Zack took out the money. He gave them 3000; and gave me my 3000.

Yes a stupid move; but it was just beginning of a string of stupid moves I made to keep the house standing; and to keep us living at the level that we were.

To not get that 7000 was a big blow, I was really expecting it. From memory though this was the first bonehead move of the New Year, I took that 3000 though, and melted it into the household.

We were making it; looking like 1 million bucks. Looking like that duck swimming smooth underwater. Underneath just like those duck feet's; I was a hustler. My duck feet were pedaling like hell.

About four months went by when I got a call from Zack. He said that he couldn't afford the Range Rover payments anymore. The payments were about $500 each month. He came down to my house; from Sacramento. He dropped the vehicle off at my house. I had to accept this. I really wasn't expecting this; but there it was back at me, dropped off in my lap.

I tried to keep an even keel. As time move forward I had to think of things to do with the situation. My credit was all that I had. It was nice for bragging rights to have that Range Rover parked in my driveway. I even took some strange looks from my neighbor who was obviously a jealous man. I guess seeing a Range Rover in my driveway made him take a look at his meager existence; and produce hateful looks toward me. I took it in stride, did not make any waves, and just knew I had a jealous neighbor.

So now at this time, I had a wheelchair van, a ford being financed and Tina's maverick; which was still not running right. The ford was a stick shift. I had not shown Tina how to drive a stick shift. So at that time she wasn't driving.

The Range Rover for the most part set in my driveway. Despite the prestige; I wasn't really impressed with it; because I didn't like the way the seats felt while I drove it. It just wasn't very comfortable for me.

I had to reroute what I wanted to do with this problem. I now had two car notes with no income. Tina continued to get income for her eldest son Harry; but I never messed with that money. I always let her do whatever she wanted to do with that money. For the most part she just spent it on the house and her son.

A few weeks later Zack called me and said he was ready to resume payments on the Range Rover. I was happy that this problem was going to be lifted off my back. I wasn't even mad at that time. I just wanted this problem to go away. When he drove away, I was happy.

Weeks went by and my anger brewed up inside me. I remembered when he came to pick up the vehicle; he reached under the hood and hit a switch. It turns out that he hit that switch when he brought it to me; so that It was not running at its maximum capacity. He hit that switch when he picked it up. I remember driving it after he had dropped it off and it seemed to run rough. So that's what he did! He made it run rough so that if I wanted to do something with my truck I would have to pay someone to find out what the problem was. This would have probably delayed whatever I would want to do. A real slick move, I never liked that dude anyway. Yeah I got the three grand but he had bought himself time for whatever reason.

My anger brewed up inside of me. I needed to keep this house afloat.

I come up with an idea. I went back to the bay. I stepped to the credit union and took out $3000 more on that range rover which raised his payments. He found out about it when he went to make his payment.

Yeah, that $3000 was much needed. I melted into the house so we kept eating, drinking and living well. That move also would come back to haunt me; but that was $3000 in the pocket and no one was going to take it away from me; nobody!

1999 was moving forward. I bought a 1989 Cadillac. That car ran good! That car looked good also. It turned out to be Tina's car to drive.

She drove it more than I did. I still had the ford though.

She looked good driving. I was so proud of her. She looked good in everything she did. Look at my queen. I loved that woman so much! I felt proud that I had done something no other man in her life before me had done for her. I had made sure she had what I had. The fundamental ability to drive a car; and not only to drive; but to have full access to any car she could drive in the household.

I was rolling right now with about 1 to 2 months' worth of finances ahead of my bills. But the bills were chasing me. I had to stay grounded in my thinking, while we were living well. Continual moves had to be made to stay afloat.

I was still trying to put this transportation business together. Step by step. I was getting closer and closer to being a full-fledged owner of my own transportation company in the great city of Fresno. That was the deal, keep things up until I get this business going.

It's crazy, because a small part of the reason I came to Fresno was to get a new relationship with Mitch. That would never truly happen.

To this day at the time of his writing January 2016 we do not have the relationship I came to Fresno wanting.

Mitch worked at an irrigation company for almost 2 decades. I had a corner house. I had grass, sprinklers, flowers, everything surrounded the house. I needed his expertise. I offered to pay him of course. He kept putting me off, talking about how he would get fired if he got caught working at my house. He said his company wouldn't allow it. I saw it as a lie. I felt like what a person did on his own time, was his own time. Nobody was going to tell me I could not use my expertise to make more money, feed my family. I left him alone for a long time. I let him take his and jealousy, and keep it moving. Yeah he was probably upset also that I helped with the cooking in my own house. He felt that that made him look bad, in his household. Hell I was once a culinary arts student as readers know. I liked to cook. Therefore, since I wasn't working a 40 hour work week, why shouldn't I cook a few days a week; to help Tina out. She cooked the majority of the time; but I cooked weekly also.

Mitch didn't believe in that philosophy; which is cool. He took offense because I was making him look bad in the eyes of Laverne. I had a new business coming. I seemed to always have money; and I was breaking or even changing the manhood mold by sometimes cooking for the household. I went forward; feeling like he got a problem, I don't.

Tina drove the Catholic most of the time. I drove the ford. I was still putting the business together. We had too many vehicles. I sold the little maverick. I never did fix that thing. It served its purpose. Tina learned the initial foundation of driving in that car.

We had a lot of resources on the surface. We were treated like we were the new players in town; but I never bought into that. I just kept on hustling.

In 1999 and before, I had my cannabis card, which meant for those readers who don't know, allow me the ability to purchase and even to grow a certain amount of weed. Yeah I had gone to San Francisco to get my card.

As far as I can remember I was charged about $175, to cover one year. I drove to Visalia; which is south of Fresno. It's about a 30 to 45 minute drive. I took the Cadillac. I was rolling on the freeway. That Cadillac had been everywhere never had any problem with it. I'm rolling along on my way back; when all of a sudden the car just shut off. I pulled to the side of the freeway.

The engine was shot. It wouldn't say anything. I didn't have a cell phone on me that day; so I was in deep trouble. Cars were flying by me. It was a very hot day. That's what the Central California Valley is famous for, hundred degree days and over 100 in the summer is, common. So here I am walking down the freeway, after securing my car. Sweat was dripping off my forehead. I'm walking and walking. All of a sudden some older white man pulled up along the shoulder and asked if I needed help. If the word racist had a picture attached to it in the dictionary, I thought it had to have this man's face. He looked like he was straight out the Jim Crow era. This man stopped with a smile; and offered me a ride to the nearest exit. He took me to a gas station so I can use the phone. He even bought me some ice cream. Yeah I had money, he just offered. I said my thank yours and all that, I got my car towed home but I would never measure a man by what he looked like again.

So now the Cadillac was shot. I found out that the water pump went out; and with a 4100 engine, one gets no warning. I found out that when the water pump goes out, the engine with the aluminum casing overheats. It was over. The Cadillac was gone.

Now I needed to get my Ford back that I had let Nate use because he didn't have a car. I got in contact with him, and told him. When I got my car back though, the clutch was all messed up. It seems Nate had been letting his mate's son use the car; and he had messed up the clutch; burned it out. Wow, try to do something nice, and look at where he got me.

I got rid of the Cadillac, and shut Tina's car down until I could figure out what to do with it. I needed money quick! The sense of urgency was real.

I then did something that I'm not proud of. I still won't go into detail about it. I'll just say at this time in my life I became a hell of a hustler. This is not something I'm bragging about. I was not going to let our living standards drop. I would sit in my room with the lights down low, and contemplate how I was going to pull this off. I contemplated four hours until I came up what felt like was a full proof plan. After I came up with the plan, I switched sides and became the person who would be looking into this plan. I picked apart my plan over and over again from both sides. I was looking for loopholes, until I found no kinks in my plan.

I then made sure to keep Tina, and any of the kids out of the loop. I didn't want anybody to even think they had to question her. She didn't know anything; I was the responsible person of everything I did that was the system I used.

Although I can't go into detail, lawyers have told me even though it's been almost two decades; I could still be charged today. The only thing I can say is that I received between 4000 and $7000 dollars every time I did what I did. I did this seven times over the next few years. I was never caught.

I do want the readers to know that I did try that mess in 2011 and almost got caught up. They were waiting to wrap me up. They had evidence, of old cases, old po's and everything. I did manage to get out of it, but it was close. 2011 was my worst year while married; but we will get to that later.

As 1999 rolled along we were still living like royalty. I was still hustling, re-creating myself. Some might say why I didn't just get a job. I did not put too much stock in getting a job in Fresno; because I knew that I would not get the kind of money I was accustomed to. I came here to be a businessman. I didn't come here to work for peanuts. Fresno was not the bay. Jobs were not plentiful. This was an agricultural community. I wasn't going to work no slave wages. I was a working kind of guy. I was that guy; but Fresno, I didn't come here for that. I continued to do what I had to do.

Yes, It begin to merge fresher and fresher in my mind, that I was putting myself in many precarious positions; but I was in love. I was willing to do what I had to do. This family was going to stand; and continue to live well. I was not one to let anyone down. I was the man and I was going to stay the man. I maintained a low-key demeanor. I guess many people were probably taking my kindness for weakness; but I did not need to be all boisterous. I was laid back; that was my demeanor. I didn't need to do a lot of yelling; and loud for no reason. I was the man, and I handled my business. Few people knew for sure how I got my money. It wasn't something I bragged about. It was to be kept private.

Anyway I ended up having to get a car; actually a van. It was a Plymouth that seated seven people. Tina could drive it and all was good.

Nate at this time was showing some signs of slippage. He was showing some signs that he wasn't as sharp as he had been previous years.

It was 1999. After all he was 73 years old now.

Nate was the payee for J.R. J.R. at this time was a substance abuser for 17 years straight. Nate was handling his financial affairs. What a job; handling the affairs of someone as sick as he was the readers know, that I know, that was a hard job.

Anyway, Nate needed to go back to the bay area in order to take J.R. to the medical facility.. They needed to check him out; in order to sign the disability papers, J.R's insurance needed to continue to give him his disability check. They needed to sign the paper, so that J.R's disability check would still come in monthly. Once a year or so those papers needed to be signed, so I picked them up all on our journey, to the bay. We arrived there on time for J.R's appointment. . We sat in the waiting room. J.R had his medical appointment visit; we were getting ready to leave. It turns out they would not sign the paperwork be—cause Nate still owed the doctor some money from previous visits. When we got in my car it wouldn't start. What the hell! I'm no mechanic. All I know is that we were sitting in the car in a pickle.

Nate swung into action. He told J.R. and I to stay there.

Now in 1999 I was 38 years old. J.R., was 42 years old. Nate sprang he man hero mold, like he had always done. He had a friend in the area. He went to find a friend to get us help. The friend came and went underneath the car. The friend thought he could tap on the starter underneath the car. And get us moving. That didn't work. Time was getting later into the day. Nate told us to stay in the car again; while he took off to try his plan B. I'm a grown man, but now I'm sitting in the car for a couple of hours. What the hell was going on I thought. Now I'm starting to come up with counter plans just in case. Pops came back; but it wasn't going to happen.

Time was getting short for the day. It was getting dark. I remember pushing the car out of the office parking lot. Pushing the car onto the street was what we did.

We got out and walked. While we were walking toward the train station; we heard a train coming, stopping and going. We didn't think anything of it; except to find out that when we got to the train station that was the train we should have gotten on. We just missed it. Nate seemed a little unsure. I wanted to implement something out of my mind; but I continued to follow his lead out of respect. That's what I did; respect was constant from my upbringing. One respected his elders without question.

Nate was a little slow right then. I recognized this and started offering suggestions. I did a money check. Of course J.R. didn't have any money.

Usually, at least when I was a substance abuser, money didn't stay in my pocket very long. Money was the trigger to get me out there. Looking to get high again.. I found that we didn't have enough money left for three train tickets anyway. We got on the 7f bus. We took this bus to San Francisco. The same bus I had taken four years earlier getting away from Jake. We arrived at the San Francisco bus station. We had to wait until 4 am to catch the next bus to Fresno. Wow it was about 8 pm when we arrived at the bus station. It was cold. I was now funky. Wow what a day. We got through it; got back to Fresno. What a 24 hour period. I knew then that my pop wasn't the man mentally that he had been in earlier years. He had slow signs of the Demetria. I went back the next day.

I got to the process of getting my car fixed even though I was 200 miles away. I drove the car home. It was a fluke situation. A bolt fell off something and messed up the flywheel. I got things done though.

The queen was holding down the house every day. The house stayed clean. She cooked every day; except the days where I gave her a break.

Wow! She was a great cook too. She had it all; beauty, intelligence, caring, supporting, graceful etc. My queen! I was a very happy man, even though I had a great deal of pressure on my back. I could not and did not wilt under pressure.

I remember the legacy set by my Nate. Never did we have the lights, cut off. Never was the water cut off. We were never lacking for food and drink. God is good; and was then. God made her great. She was already there. I had to catch up. I stayed on the grind. We moved through 1999. I must remind the readers that I am writing in January 2016 at this time. I am recalling from memory.

1999 went forward, when something happened. My memory is a little fuzzy; but what happened, happened. Tina asked me if it was okay for her elder and her sibling could move in. I of course had no problem with that.

I will say that her elder was fantastic to me. My wife told me that she liked me. She just didn't like my health situation, because I was overweight. She used to kid me about that. I must have weighed about 250 pounds at that time, mentioning the weight issue, that I had most of my life.

Her elders, name was Lisa, I believe at that time was a double amputee. The same situation Teresa was in before she passed. Lisa was a very sharp, feisty woman; just like her daughter; Tina. Lisa's daughter, Tina's older sister was mentally delayed. She was a sweet woman too.

Mabel, the older sibling, was a hoarder as I found out; but that was cool too, because she hoarded her own room. Mabel as Tina told me later usually said the opposite of what she really meant. I learned to pick up, and accept her demeanor. One of her pros was that she cleaned everything in sight. She did a lot of cussing and cleaning. She cleaned all day, every day. She even cleaned in the early a.m. hours. She was fulfilling whatever project she had in mind. She would say "I am not no damn maid". One of the sayings she would say to anybody she felt was lounging was "you didn't work". She would usually tell that to the kids. Even she had learned a great work ethic. A con about her was that whenever we moved in future years, Mable would have mountains of stuff. Everyone that came to help us move was amazed at what she had managed to hoard. We just endured and dealt with that when we moved. The con that got to me was that she had a problem saying my name. In the early days she couldn't say D.L. She called me Dasia. Sounded like a woman's name to me. Everyone seemed to get a kick out of that. I don't remember what year she was able to say my name; but she did; thank God!

Mabel and Lisa settled into the household as we got to approach the year 2000.

I remember everyone was very apprehensive. There was talk of the end of time, the end of life as we knew it. There was the Y2K, or whatever that was a scare. It was said that the computers were going to malfunction.

They said the world was in trouble etc.

Yes some of that stuff got to me also. Yet I still had to maintain the status quo. Now I had two more people in the household that I had to provide safety and protection. I did my job!

Finances were getting low again. Bills were creeping into my 90 day protection zone. That was my margin of error. I once heard that a person should have at least 90 days' worth of resources to cover three months' worth of bills. That became my standard. No one knew but me.

Tina never knew about that part because although she was just as capable as myself; she let me do the budget.

Lisa controlled Mabel's finances; and I believe gave Tina money for rent. I never knew what Lisa gave her; or even if anything was given at all.

Whatever it was, If It was, I did not make it my concern. I didn't make that my business. I stayed in my lane on that one; although whatever it was it went to my wife finances. Mabel and Lisa was protected and comfortable.

I needed to make another move. I wasn't close to getting my business up and running. It takes a lot of money and time to be a Medi-Cal provider.

That was what I was shooting for; but I wasn't close right then.

I had to get more money! I decided to get a second loan on the house.

At this time I had two auto loans on my credit. The ford had not gotten fixed yet. That was one of the vehicles; including the Range Rover; but Zack was paying for that.

I remember sitting in my little think tank, my bedroom, my office. I went in there, turned the lights down low, and sought to make it happen. I was on the phone for hours and hours trying to get some money to keep this thing going. When the business day ended, my quest ended that day. I pursued this venture daily; with no success. I was not dismayed. I was not discouraged.

One day I was at my business, and finished the business day, I thought successfully. I was getting a newspaper delivered then; the Fresno bee. Tina went outside in the early morning; perhaps seven or 8 AM. She went out after five year old Earl was dropped off at school. She came back in the house, I was drinking my coffee. I was getting ready to get back on the grind. Tina went outside to get the newspaper, and came in with a next day air package. We took it inside and there was $25,000 worth of checks.

We were ecstatic. I knew I had finalized that initial loan for the house in the first place. Now I got an additional $25,000. I knew I had to pay a lot of back bills. I also knew this brought me a lot of time. I knew I could relax a little bit. I paid back some of the bills that were crowding me; and moved forward; looking forward to the year 2000!

CHAPTER 11

The year 2000

IT WAS TIME TO party! It was New Year's Eve 1999. Everyone was a little amped; and a little apprehensive. The talk amongst the media and in the general school of thought was about the collapse of the computers. The year 2000 was coming. Y2K was in effect. Whatever the hell that meant. Even with the negative bull that the establishment had put on most people's minds; including myself. The party was going to happen on schedule. I purchased a video camera; so I could get great footage. Great footage I did get. Everyone was in a festive mood. I barbecued that morning.

I had plenty of meat. Tina made her world famous mac & cheese. Potato salad was off the hook. Everybody can't make good potato salad. Tina was a hell of a cook. Potato salad was an easy fix for her. She also made collard greens, jambalaya and many other fixings. We had big pots for big eaters. I was preparing a video camera; getting used to working it. My wife and two of her kids handled the music. Her two kids, Terry and Nancy I believe handled the music. Nancy was about 17 I believe. Harry was the cutest kid one ever saw, the little guy with the long hair.

I used to tell him that his hair was bigger than he was.

I interrupt the party talk to mention to the readers one situation that stayed with me. A year earlier while I was courting my woman; Harry walked up and set between us and told me to call him son. That was one of the warmest, and at the same time, most shocking situation, that I was not expecting. I had no off-spring.

Tina was done having kids; so that's what it was. I need to say at this writing in 2016; that, that young man grew with great integrity. He is months away from graduating Fresno city College. I am so proud of him. But he had a foundation of love that never faltered.

Anyway back to the party. It was New Year's Eve 1999. 2000, 00, party over, oops out of time, I'm going to party like its 1999. The Prince Song was ringing in many people's ears. Everyone held the hope, the promise of 2000. Yet the Y2K scare was still in people's minds. I think the fact about the Y2K and the significance of year 2000, coming in was huge. I think it actually fueled the party. The people started coming in. The house was filling up; wow! What a turnout! I don't know what other parties were going on; but ours was the place to be. I would imagine, Tina's whole Fresno family was there. It was packed. We had loads of food. We had all kinds of drinks. We were stacked up with food; and I had plenty of herbs. That's a California foundation. I had my sack of that good sticky. I believe I had Kush. Oh yeah we were ready! I started smoking weed at two years clean.

The house was filling up. The music was loud; and there became standing room only. I had my garage open also. That was my man cave. That's where I smoked my trees on break time. I switched the locks around on the garage door, the kitchen door. You had to have a key to go from the kitchen to the garage. That way I could separate myself from the young kids when I smoked my trees.

I opened the man cave for those friends who wanted to smoke.

Packed, packed, and packed! It had to be all her family in Fresno like I said.

Even some of my few family members showed up. Teresa's sibling James, he's gone to glory now. Even he showed up. He stood 6 foot three. He was a retired construction worker. At this time he had to be in his late 70s. He was still a party animal. I can see him in my mind right now; cutting a rug. He was a heavy drinker; but he handled his liquor well. Not everyone of course can say that.

What a party! We partied, ate, drank, and smoked throughout the pm hours; heading into the midnight time. No anger, no gunplay, just pure, honest fun going on. I even got on the floor to cut a rug; and I'm no dancer; but I was that night! I strolled around the house with the videocam, and caught everybody. I made people speak into the camera. I got a lot of good footage. At this writing time, January 2016, I will get the footage put on a disk, so that those loved ones can see the ones who were at that party; that are no longer here right now.

The party moved forward. We did the countdown. We were happy, partying, eating, drinking and having a good time. As the party spilled past midnight, into the early a.m. a strange thing happened, life went on. The year 2000 was here; and no one was going to take it away from us. The world didn't stop spinning. All the Y2K talk, was just that, talk. We had made it and I was happy. The party had been a success. I may be bias; but it was the best party I have ever been to; and to this day still the best.

I knew what I was in for now. Wow what a year. I got to relax a little bit for a few months; but the grind was always on. I had a second mortgage now. I still had little income coming in. I had to get that business up and running. I put more and more of my time into getting my business up and running. It is a very tedious process becoming a California Medi-Cal provider.

The first process is getting the van. Of course I already had that. The van needs to be tight and right. It has to have a rubber floor board in case someone throws up. So that it can be easily cleaned. No carpet is allowed in the areas that the passengers will be riding in. Of course the registration must be up-to-date. One needs the normal business license and fictitious name statement. The application to California Medi-Cal is understandable; but pretty complex as to what they want. Everything must be done exactly the way they want. The application, when turned in must have full coverage insurance. They want million-dollar coverage for the auto insurance.

The application usually takes about three months to be viewed by Medi-Cal. The insurance costed a $400 down payment; and about $300 per month. The insurance has to be in effect while the application is being reviewed. Therefore even though I didn't have any clients; I still had to have insurance in place; while the application was being reviewed. I finally had the application filled out with insurance in force. It was a very lengthy and expensive process. But now, I had my application sent in. I just had to maintain the status quo.

The year 2000 went forward and I was making sure everything stayed afloat as usual.

Yeah money was blowing out the house like crazy. There was really the process of just maintaining the regular bills going on, but now I had a second mortgage. I was still staying ahead of my bills, with my three months emergency program. But bills were creeping in with no income coming in.

I did make what turned out to be a mistake. I got some storm windows put onto the house. It gets extremely hot in Fresno during the summer. The storm windows I installed really helped with the heat coming through the house from the outside.

Those storm windows really amounted to another mortgage though. They wanted their money.

We still lived well, and that was the overriding factor. I saw my pops do it for our family growing up. I was going to keep it going for mine. I knew the way I was living was very unconventional; very dangerous, and very stressful. I just figured that getting that business started would change everything. Then I would have the income I needed to take care of the bills coming in every day.

I was no fool, just living above my means because I could. I had a plan. At the same time I was improvising like crazy. I was making it happen like a Captain. I handled my business with a sense of urgency; because I carried everybody in the house, in my heart.

Months were going by in the year 2000. My income was still not right. I continued to push my potential business to make sure I had all my p's and q's in line.

The bank was starting to squeeze me. I could see it coming. I had so many things on my credit now. I had a mortgage, a second mortgage, a $50,000 Range Rover, $12,000 ford and about 8 to 9 credit cards. I remember needing to go back to the credit union to get some more money. I had a feeling that the well I was going to run dry. I arrived in the bay area. My three month bill barrier was being threatened. I stepped into the credit union lobby. My thoughts turned to a time just one year ago.

When Tina and I were staying in Redwood City, I would take her to the bank with extreme confidence. We would sit in the car and I would tell her, that I betted her that I would get $5,000. I always got what I wanted.

This time though, I was not that optimistic. I had had enough dealings to know that the bank was getting tight. I used to come into the bank and the manager would greet me with "hello Mr. King, how are you doing Mr. King?" Julie cut Mr. King a check for 2000, 5000, or whatever I needed. Wow those were the days. But this was not those days and I knew it.

I walked in as usual. I sat down, ready to see the bank manager. They did not seem as happy to see me. Of course I got turned down for my $3900 loan request. It seemed my credit report was packed. It wasn't a problem that I wasn't paying my loans. The problem was my credit report was packed to the max.

I returned home knowing I had to do something; because my three month barrier was being threatened. I had about three months' worth of financing to live on. I was in the red zone. I had to figure it out.

I needed to get back in the think tank. My think tank was my bedroom. I would go in there, dim the lights, turn off all noise and basically become one with my mind.

This day it was about 1 pm. I was in the think tank. Tina was buzzing around the house looking like the queen that she was. Maybe the readers will understand the pressure I put on myself to keep the queen happy; to keep the queen laced with whatever she wanted. That's that real love!

The door was closed. My mind was concentrating. My eyes were closed. I had to get that $3900; I was thinking. I must get it. My eyes slowly opened. I thought "don't I continue to make payments on that ford outside?" What if I told them I needed the $3900 to fix the engine of the car that I am financing from them? Chances are that I would get that loan. Why would they deny me an opportunity to fix their car, basically was my premise. My thinking was clear and my logic was sound.

When I say my thinking was clear. My thinking was clear. I never mixed business with pleasure. I didn't smoke or what I called take my medication, when I handled my business. This went back to never getting high before school.

I went back to the bank with my new plan in mind. I followed the same routine; even though Julie the secretary wasn't coming at me with coffee and donuts anymore; but that was okay. I just wanted that money. Well, I told them my spill. I sat down and waited. I thought I had them in a bind. I was a little more optimistic this time.

The manager came out with a strange look on his face. What happened to his smile? Where's Julie with the coffee and donuts. There was no Julie and no smile. The manager told me was that the bank would cut the check for the loan; but the check would only be cut to the name of the mechanic. Wow, I at least got half of what I wanted. I had to tweak this, back to the think tank. My first thoughts were "how do I find a mechanic I can trust to do this? Dam! How much of my money would I have to give this mystery man?" I did not like the situation. I had money I could get from the bank; but it wasn't going to be in my name.

Just like that think and grow rich book back in 1994, in detox; I had to get past this problem. This was my latest and greatest obstacle.

I just want to take a second and get off script a little bit. Thinking back I really was not conscious of the fact, or even thinking about the fact that just a few years back I was a very sick man. Now I'm counting thousands monthly. I really didn't even think about that at the time. It's almost like I was supposed to be rolling with this kind of money.

Lawyers have warned me not to put in this manuscript the things I did. They told me I should not mention some of the hustles I did to keep things popping. The fact is I had to transform myself to a hustler. I was still a cool square; but that's the rub. I was able to hustle in areas no one expected me to be in. No one saw me coming. No one saw me leave. But I wasn't a burglar. Let's just say I got my hands on that $3900 legally.

Meanwhile on the home front, Tina was impeccable inside the house.

She had such great taste. It looked like we stepped out of a magazine inside my house. Everything was new and fresh. Everyone was doing well. Everyone seemed happy. That was important to me. I was happy, that I bought myself more time.

Tina took care of the house. She took care of the kids. She took care of Lisa and Mabel. She also took care of me. She was my queen and I was her man. We were living like low key royalty and my job was to keep it going.

I do want to make it clear to the readers that Tina, except for the initial furnishing of the house; in no way pushed me into the extravagance we were living. I did what I did because I threw away so many years of my life. I wanted to make up for lost time. I wanted the best of everything. I was willing to do whatever I had to do; without physically harming anyone; and that's what I did. When I got the queen! That was the last piece of the puzzle. It was on now. We continued to live well. I was stressed the hell out. But we continued to live like royalty. We just started off with so much; I wanted to keep it going. I felt like I deserved it; and so did she. I knew that getting that business off the ground was going to sustain everything!

I needed to keep everything up and running. Yeah it was a hard job. But somebody had to do it. I was a man;. I was the guy. I had a queen and she deserved it all!

I was in the waiting period for Medi-Cal. I had two weeks relaxation. I was thinking about the stressful financial situation because I knew I had a couple weeks to get my mind relaxed little bit.

I was still doing my thing. My lawyers told me not to mention hustles. I was still bringing in thousands, but it was the type of situation that I had to be perfect to get my money. I was perfect for seven different times. My hustles brought in between 4000 and $7000 each time. But as time went on, my adversaries got smarter, I eventually had to retire from doing what I did. Say no more!

The year 2000 moved forward. We all seemed happy; all six people in the household. Lisa was getting a little sickly though.

We went forward living like giants. I needed to keep making financial moves while Medi-Cal was reviewing my application. Keeping finances coming in continued to be job number one. As it should have been, all the other things though, had to be done; as well as being a provider. But yes provider was about 80% of what I did. I know I had some shortcomings in the other areas. But just like Nate had laid the foundation within me, years ago; now it was my turn. I wasn't going to let anybody down! At the same time getting locked up was not a part of my grand plan. The grand plan in of itself was simple.

Hold up the family on my shoulders until the Medi-Cal provider application was approved. Then I was going to get into something I knew well. Being a Medi-Cal provider, transporting seniors, and the handicapped to dialysis and other medical appointments.

As things went forward in the year 2000 the overhead of the house finances were creeping upward. I was probably spending over $4000 a month.

It never came to my mind to consult Tina about new ways to bring cash into the house. I never had that discussion. I took it upon my shoulders. I took that responsibility. When I married her, I told her she didn't have to work. She did work though. She was the homemaker. She kept that house tight and clean. She took care of the kids, Lisa, Mabel and everyone else in her presence. God's angel she was. She worked and worked hard.

Lisa was getting even more sickly. She was having breathing problems. Tina knew what the doctor told her; that Lisa didn't have much time left. Medical people told my wife that the most likely scenario would be that Lisa would pass away in her sleep. Tina did not discuss that with me at the time. She kept that information inside of her. God only knows what pressure that knowledge was inside of her. I don't know, maybe she discussed it with her siblings. My wife had I believe 7 siblings.

Time went forward to the point where I had to get a third loan on the house.

The third was much harder to get then the second. With a lot more harsher terms, I would not suggest that move on anyone. Things were really intense now. Three mortgages over my head with little income. Things were intense indeed. I only got $7000 for the third mortgage. It was just a drop in the bucket at this time.

I was seeing that my three months' worth of security had dropped to two months and kicking the hell out of one and a half months security. I had to keep things of float, which I did; but moves were getting harder and harder to find at this time. I was still waiting for medical to approve me. I was still carrying full coverage business insurance at a rate of about $300 per month; although I wasn't carrying any passengers. I now had a first, second and third mortgage; and I got them storm windows which was actually constituted a fourth loan on the house.

We were not living very extravagant at this time. No we weren't. Things had settled down to the point that we were living good. Yes, but things were getting intense in terms of finances. No one really knew but me. I didn't want to bring any bad news to Tina.

I knew she had enough worries, cares and concerns taking care of Lisa, Mabel and the kids.

A good person, homemaker, mate, sibling, and on and on and on, I must be honest with the readers. This started off as a tribute to the greatest love I ever had, but it really will be a testimony of what one man did. Excuse me what one man did to keep his queen safe and secure. Everyone who knew Tina knew what kind of person she was. This is the truth. This is the history. This is what happened over seventeen years. Some would want to erase me and dumb me down. Erase me even though this book is the truthful history and testimony of what happened. This book is also a testimony of how great and wonderful she was.

Back to the story, yeah, things were getting pretty intense for me. I really had to continue to make it happen.

A few more months went by. What happened next was what one would call crunch time.

The bills were now forty five days away from crushing me and my family. I knew major moves were going to have to be made in the near future in order to stay afloat; medical needed to call me quick.

I wanted to get some real nice DADA tennis shoes for Tina and myself.

I had all my checks for bills sent out for the month. I did my math as usual. All twenty something checks went out and were covered by the money I had in the bank. I ordered the DADA tennis shoes for Tina and me. I think the bill came up to about $234. The shoes came.

She loved them and I loved them. The problem was that some rookie that took my order doubled the order. Therefore what was a $234 bill became a $468 bill. All the checks I had written were bouncing out the bank. I'm getting notices left and right.

The bank was charging me $35 per check in the overdraft system. I had busted it wide open. I tried to contact DADA to reverse the charges but things were too late. The gig was up. I was severely overdrawn and I was in trouble.

I would have brought another month worth of security had it not been for that mistake.

But it was what it was I knew I had to move.

It started to dawn on me that now I was in a very precarious position. We were in a precarious position. I had to act fast. After all I had done a bunch of hustles. I was on the hot seat. I had to get my family to safety. I wasn't going to be able to be the provider I imagined myself sitting in a cell. We had to move. Medical at this time had not called yet. My big remedy for the whole income situation was not yet in my hands. We had to go and go fast. I had to tell Tina.

Tina, what a woman; so supportive. Had to rent a U-Haul and move everything. I really didn't focus on the whole situation from start to finish. Looking back today I missed a lot of opportunities. I held out for the ultimate. A real live income in Fresno. I never came to Fresno to work for someone else. I came to be a business owner. That was my aim and that's what I set out to do.

Looking back at the whole situation, I can honestly say that I was the ultimate provider to this point. I had done what Nate done before me. At least I didn't let anyone down and I took $3000 and carried out a one and a half year existence. Yeah I went through a lot of money, but income is essential. At this point I was the establishment's financial nightmare. I had gotten what I wanted from the banks, hoodwinked another industry, and carved out a living for my family and my queen. One has to realize that I was only two and a half years clean after over 12 years of madness.

This is a love story that kept going on. Yea I could have cut out and bounced when the going was a little rough; and I received that $25,000 as many men would have done. I honestly never considered it at all. I was in love, nose wide open as the old folks would say. Yes my nose was wide open. I loved my queen and would do anything I needed to do in order to keep her safe and secure.

We moved to a house in sort of East Central Fresno. It was nothing to write home about. It was just a house like any other house, nothing special.

We moved in and I was still waiting from notification from Medical. I switched all the new information regarding my new address. It was a process that slowed things down some more, which of course I did not need.

Everyone was doing well except Lisa. She was still sickly.

From memory I can say that we stayed as homeowners for about one and half years before moving.

We were settling into a four bedroom house. Lisa had her own room again. Mabel had her own room. The two young men had their own room and of course Tina and I. I was putting down all anchors, making sure everything outside the house was taken care of. I need to mention that never did she show or speak any negativity to me, totally supportive. Wow, that woman a real woman backing her man. She understood all the work I put into make sure everyone was in good standing.

A few weeks went by and everything was pretty stabilized. Our income was still an issue, of course. Things were a little bit more manageable with not having to pay literally four mortgages. WOW things were much easier, but I wasn't out of the woods yet.

Those few weeks turned into the next month. I had turned over everything at the time that I was willing to do. The next hustle, at this time, was not in front of me. I had to space these things out. I had no more leverage at the bank. I had no street hustle that I was willing to put into play at this time. I really went for hard hitting moves. I once again needed to do something fast.

I began to rationalize and take a look at any assets I could liquidate. I then made a terrible conscious decision. I decided under the circumstances to sell my wheelchair van. Obviously I did not think it through all the way. Yeah, that was supposed to be the future. That was my number one project. I had set everything in place in order to seize the opportunity.

To be that business man in Fresno was about to disappear, the overriding reason I made the decision that I did, was part pride, part survival, and part stupidity. The problem was that bills were coming fast and I could not let the household down. I had to sell that van to buy us perhaps two more months. Part of my rationale was the fact that I had only paid $1500 for the van. I had an old couple who paid me $4000 cash. I had to do it. I had to take it. In retrospect I should have asked everyone in the household to eat sandwiches; and squeeze into, we can't pay this, no we can't get that mode. Yes in retrospect I should have done this for the big picture scheme of things. I had no idea how long Medi-cal was going to take, and they were not talking. Had to make probably one of the worst moves, worse decisions I had to make. I didn't ask anyone to squeeze in. I didn't ask anyone to contribute more. I still didn't want any drop in our standard of living. That's what I wanted. I wanted continual stability $4000 wow. I had sold our future but I had saved our present. That was the sacrifice; that was the deal. I sold that van to keep us afloat.

People years later would often point back to me selling the van. Nobody seemed to understand what was at stake. If I had let the standard of living drop, I would have gotten a lot of negative comments about the living standards. Especially with my Lisa in the house, I did what I did at the time. I made a conscious decision to keep the standard of living going, should have asked everybody to make cut backs in retrospect.

Literally two weeks later, Medi-cal called me and told me my application was approved.

They needed to get a time from me so they could come to inspect my van.

Talk about being devastated. To say the least it took a lot out of me that I had stopped two weeks short of gold. I had gone to the finish line and lost my shoe, but like the movies when the monster comes some woman always lost her shoe. That's exactly how I felt. Not like a woman of course. I felt like I stopped two weeks short of gold.

Just like in the think and grow rich book, back in 1994, at detox. There was a story of a guy from the east coast that came west for the gold rush. He sold everything of value he had. He borrowed money from family and friends. He came west to mine for gold. As I remember the story he put his time in mining for gold. He had great energy and ambition like I did. He was persistent day after day mining for gold. Just like me, persistently hustling to keep my family afloat. He kept on day after day for months.

He really did not get much gold; at least enough to justify his quest. He sold his equipment to an old geezer from the area. He went back home a failure. Now much in debt, he had to find a way to pay back family and friends and to regain his foundation. He sold the mining equipment to this old geezer who had the sense to hire a surveyor. The surveyor did his work and found a vein of gold just two feet away from where the young man from the east coast had dug. The geezer moved over and started mining in that new area and became a very rich man. The man from the east coast had stopped, quit just two feet short of gold. And that was the story I read back in that book; thing and grow rich back in 1994. This for me, is a much similar was situation. I stopped two weeks short of gold.

To get that call was a devastating blow. It really took the wind out of my sails deeply. I could not get that van back even though lord knows I wish I could. I had to live with that. I had to own it. All in all what was done was done. I still had the responsibility target on my back. I had to pull myself up and carry on.

From memory it had to be less than 2-3 weeks later that something else happened.

It was like any other morning; Tina awoke and did her homemaker thing.

She was good; very good. She kept a clean house; took care of everyone and everything in that house. She woke up and stepped to her Lisa's room as usual. Lisa was a double amputee; therefore Tina was on her job early and often. After all, that was her Lisa.

This morning Lisa didn't answer the call. Lisa had passed away in her sleep; just as Tina was told what might happen.

Tina screamed out in anguish. I came rushing to see what was going on. Lisa had passed. Wow! This was real. This was new. This was terrible. Tina's family was notified. All her siblings were present. I believe except "E" who will be talked about later; and Paul, who lived out of state.

Her oldest sibling Pete was there. I believe her siblings Tootie and Lettie were there. Her son Harry of course was there. And her younger sibling Ms. Sincere was also there. Terry came by. Most of all Tina's immediate family was there, including Nancy. Also Mabel was already there, including the young seven year old. The living room was full of grief. The matriarch was gone. Sorrow and grief filled the air. I now a married man for a year and a half; maintained the only role I could muster. I had to be supportive, a host, a confidant, a positive person to help in any way I could; in this time of grief. What a terrible situation. This was definitely new to me as a mate.

Although I was an in-law, there were no in-laws or outlaws that morning. We were all there for one purpose only, to try to console each other in light of this great loss.

What a moment. Yeah, well that was just the beginning. I flashed in and out of the bedroom. I wanted to sit in there and console and grieve with the rest of the family; but I came in and out, because I really didn't want to remain in the living room consistently with the uneasiness going on between Nancy and myself.

Nate and Teresa were both raised in the South. Tina's people were raised in the South also. Tina was raised on the East Coast. I was raised on the West Coast.

We had one great thing in common among other things. She and I were both raised with the old school foundation. The black folks from this era, the older ones such as I, Tina and my parent's age were raised with tremendous respect for elders. Older black folks that were born in the 20's, 30's etc., in the Jim Crow era, respect was an underlying foundation. We had great respect; Tina and I, for our elders. We both were raised with that foundation even though we were from two different coasts. That Southern foundation was engraved within us. We never left it. We paid our dues. Now we were either in our late 30's or early 40's. Now was time to get our respect. We paid our dues, but somehow the generations behind us lost that foundation. This animosity between her daughter and me was just too much to deal with that morning. If arguments came up between Nancy and me; I didn't want to have to deal with that, if I did not have too. That is why I flowed back and forth from the bedroom to the living room to block some of the possibility that Nancy and I might get into it. I screwed up; because if I had stayed in the front room consistently I might have been able to see, and possibly stop, the great spirited young man Harry, who guzzled a bottle of liquor, that had been placed in the freezer to chill. Harry, having got a hold of it in the kitchen while nobody noticed. Guzzled the liquor and passed out dying, with vomit coming out of his mouth. I could have been in there with another pair of eyes.

I should have been in there. I wasn't. Nobody was in the kitchen except Harry. No one knows how long he was passed out on the kitchen floor. Tina heard the water running in the sink, in the kitchen; and asked Pete to cut it off. Pete cut the water off, and it was he, who found his young nephew. What devastation. Pete tried to give him mouth to mouth. Nothing but vomit was in his mouth, and his windpipe. Harry passed that day also.

I can still remember my Tina crying for her Lisa; screaming and crying for her son. I remember myself trying to console her. The whole family in that house was devastated.

Terry took things very hard; for he left the liquor in the freezer. Everyone was heartbroken. It was truly a devastating day. I remember ambulance, firemen, and ultimately the coroner came and took Lisa's body.

There was still a chance, a small chance for Harry. Waiting in the surgery waiting room was painful for everyone; especially Tina. What a blow! What a kick in the teeth. I did the best I could to console her, but I knew it took a lot out of her. She was still a strong woman though; and she had a man that was going to stick by her side no matter what. We were a team and we were going to make it. It still wasn't the same not having Henry around. I loved that little guy.

Earl had lost his best friend, his older big buddy. Truly a tremendous lost for all. Tina, and her siblings, had lost their Lisa. It really took a long time just getting back and trying to grab a hold of some sort of semblance of life. There was no script for this one here.

We had the funeral, and buried Lisa and Harry, together in the same plot double casket and double grave.

The year 2000 had started out with the Y2K and all that talk, but what a great party. It seemed like everything went downhill from there. Having to give up my home and move.

Now losing Lisa and my step son, we all went forward with grief and heavy hearts. A few weeks later, after the funeral; Tina and I were contemplating the future.

We had the life insurance money and were regrouping. I remember one day Terry and Nancy were over to the house. They were, it seemed to me, claiming insurance money, because they were his siblings.

When I met Tina I had an insurance policy in place already. I added her on. She became a rider on my policy as well as Harry. So when the insurance company paid off we were still in grief and kind of in shock.

There was rising aggression, agitation, and frustration tied to the grief. Tina stood up and explained to them that they had not paid any premiums. Therefore they were not entitled to make any decisions whatsoever of what to do with anything. I remember giving them a thousand dollars each. I also remember Terry coming back a few days later and I remember his exact words stating "That thousand dollars wasn't anything." Terry made his money on the streets; a little bit of this and a little bit of that. He was definitely a street guy. He didn't have any education past high school. He was a street hustler.

There were natural disconnections between us. First of all was age. I was 20 years his senior. I was never the street person he was. I made my mark in other areas. I put 12 years in on the streets. I paid my dues.

That wasn't my thing. Terry was always a good idea guy though. He would always come to me with; it seemed like good business ideas.

He always kept his ear to the streets. I did not ever take up one of his ideas. It seems I was always caught up with something else that was consuming my time and finances. I wish I had taken up one of those ideas though. We did have a decent relationship in that respect. He was my ear to what was going on at any time on the streets, even though I didn't want to venture out there again.

Nancy and I never clicked. It all goes back to that respect situation. I just wasn't going to be talked to and addressed like she seemed to do everyone. I wasn't the one. We didn't do it that way in the Bay, respect with no respect comes no dialogue. At the same time I always hoped we could be civil.

Months went forward, the grief, the pain, subsided somewhat; but that was huge. Wow losing one's loved one including their son on the same day I wouldn't wish that on anyone.

We decided to move. We moved to a brand new house in Easton; which I believe is a little east of Fresno. Yes the house had only been built recently. We were the only people that had ever lived there. It was an excellent dwelling. Easton was kind of countrified. The owners were the only other house on the block at the end. Our house was at the corner. Those were the only two houses on the block. There was no grass grown yet. One could see the brand newness of the area. Two brand new houses surrounded by dirt, yet to be finished landscaping.

The owner, a woman, retired school teacher was an African American woman, perhaps 20 years older than Tina; but she was a professional woman; much in the light, I anticipated Tina being, at her age. She seemed to me like an older version of what Tina could be in a business sense.

Anyway this woman saw some of the qualities I seen in Tina. She impressed that woman to the point that the woman interviewed no one else for the rental. We got it quickly, because of Tina's impression. I knew it before we went to talk to the woman.

I used that often. I was a man that had no problems putting her out there, as the face of our relationship. She was all that; and everybody that come into contact with her knew it. I often wondered, but never asked her what it must have felt like always being the best looking woman in the room throughout her life. Like I said, Tina was one of the women in life that didn't have to wear makeup. She put on lipstick and that's all. She just rolled on looking gorgeous.

I liked and Tina loved that house. It was a three bedroom, two bath house and was huge.

The year 2000 was now slowly coming to a close. I wanted to do something special for her. So I went to an auction in Kerman, CA which was perhaps an hour and a half north of us. About half the distance between Fresno and the Bay Area, we had Tootie with us to be an extra driver. I purchased I believe it was a 1996 Lexus big body. It had all the bells and what nots, a queen of a car for my queen. It was my first auction. I bided for it and got it for her. I drove it back home while Tootie drove our car. Wow, I loved driving that car and she did too. I purchased me a car too. It was not as nice as her car. I purchased a 1992 Ford. I should have stopped there. But I also purchased an 1988 convertible BMW. That was my car, because Tina could not drive a stick.

We had money left. We had solitude with a great nice new house. We were still grieving the losses of the loved ones, but we had each other. We had love, and as we watched the year 2000 fade away; we were optimistic about our future.

CONCLUSION:

Looking back through the Crack from Crack fiend to Millionaire God Let Him Live

God let him live .... That's the conclusion: A troubled child looking for answers; looking for himself, looking for love. I went down a road that many did not come back from. God let me live when I was flying off the hills in San Francisco Hunters Point; with faulty brakes; followed and passed by bullets, after ripping off the drug dealers again. If one bullet flowed different, toward the left or the right, that would have been good night.

God let me live .... When J.R. and I rented out the room, for others to smoke crack in, when a disturbance occurred, I stuck my head in the door. He came out angry at her. Thinking I was in on whatever occurred; he shoved the knife forward toward my gut! God made him miss!

God let me live .... When my fiendish ass went outside ten minutes before midnight on New Year's night, in a crack city, to get a ten dollar rock: I gave the woman the money. He was supposed to give me the rock. Before he gave it to me, he pulled out a gun. He pointed it to my temple. He asked her "make sure its ten dollars"? If it aint ten dollars I will blow this nigga away. God let me live that day! I guess he didn't mean it. But people die that way every day.

God let me live …. When I went to crack city with a hundred dollar bill, I pulled up in the car, the guy came back with a long Clint Eastwood gun and put it to my jaw. If I had not hit the accelerator, I would not be writing this book.

God let me live! A young man finds himself. A young man finds favor from God. He is allowed to marry a Queen! The woman of his dreams.

How fortunate indeed! A young man becomes as man.

God indeed! Let him live….

Is it time to get my money?

Or is it time to payback?

Look for the next installment "Looking back at the King and Queen!"